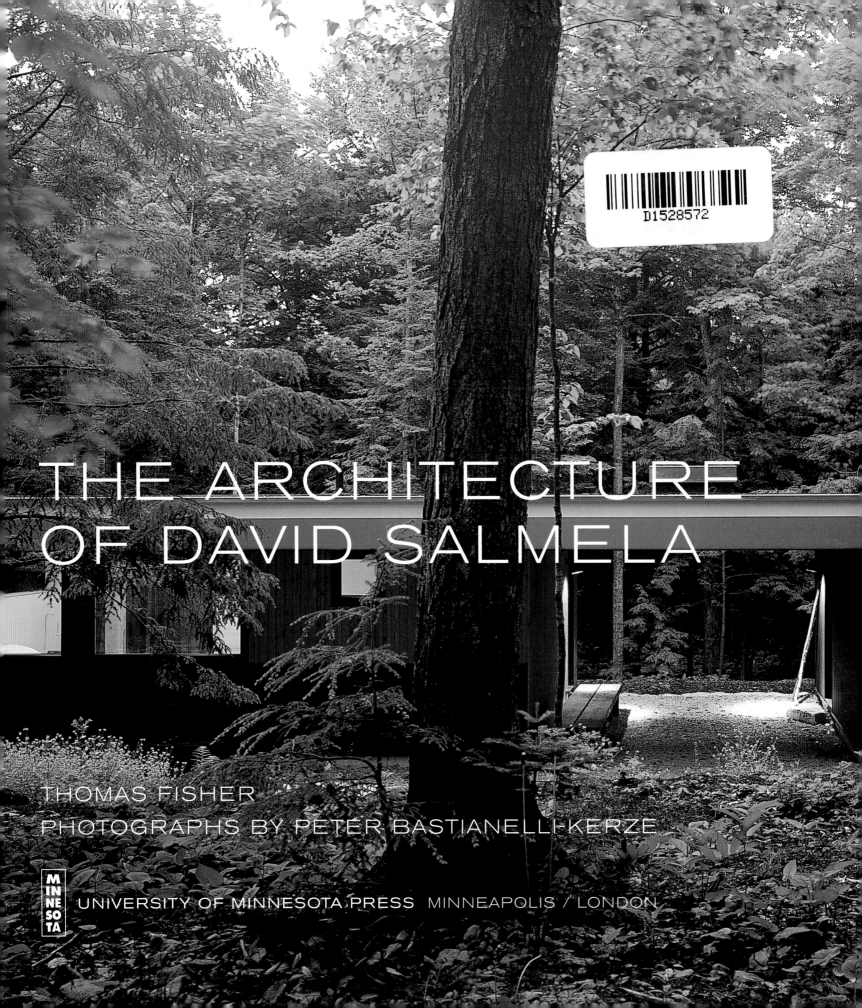

THE ARCHITECTURE OF DAVID SALMELA

THOMAS FISHER

PHOTOGRAPHS BY PETER BASTIANELLI-KERZE

UNIVERSITY OF MINNESOTA PRESS MINNEAPOLIS / LONDON

"Anecdote of Men by the Thousand" from *The Collected Poems of Wallace Stevens,* by Wallace Stevens, copyright 1954 by Wallace Stevens and renewed 1982 by Holly Stevens. Reprinted by permission of Alfred A. Knopf, a division of Random House, Inc.

Excerpt from "Evangeline: A Tale of Arcadie," by Henry Wadsworth Longfellow, was originally published by Houghton Mifflin and Company by The Riverside Press in Cambridge, Massachusetts, 1894.

Quotation from "Luminous Night," by Louis Simpson, originally appeared in *Selected Poems* (New York: Harcourt, Brace and World, 1965).

Book design by Jena Sher

Architectural model photographs and plans courtesy of Salmela Architect.

Photographs on pages 46–50, 55–59, 114–17, 152–54, and 174–78 courtesy of Salmela Architect.

Architectural plans on pages 231 and 235 courtesy of Coen + Partners.

Copyright 2011 by Thomas Fisher and David Salmela

Photographs copyright 2011 by Peter Bastianelli-Kerze unless otherwise noted.

Published by University of Minnesota Press
111 Third Avenue South, Suite 290
Minneapolis, MN 55401-2520
http://www.upress.umn.edu

Library of Congress
Cataloging-in-Publication Data

Fisher, Thomas.
*The Invisible Element of Place :
the Architecture of David Salmela /*
Thomas Fisher / Peter Bastianelli-Kerze.
   pages   cm
ISBN 978-0-8166-6993-6 (pb : alk. paper)
1. Salmela, David—Criticism and interpretation.
2. Salmela, David—Catalogs. 3. Architect-designed houses. I. Salmela, David. II. Title.
   NA737.S317F56 2011
   720.92—dc22

                         2010042825

Printed in China on acid-free paper

The University of Minnesota is an equal-opportunity educator and employer.

18 17 16 15 14 13 12 11
10 9 8 7 6 5 4 3 2 1

The University of Minnesota Press gratefully acknowledges financial assistance provided for this book by the Imagine Fund for the Arts, Design, and Humanities, an annual award from the University of Minnesota Provost's Office, and from the following individuals:

Arlin and Marilyn Albrecht
John and Mary Anderson
David and Judy Arvold
Judy Dayton
Gary and Linda Deloia
Robert Elliott
Jaiyur Hsu
Brian and Lisa Krause
David and Kathy Matthew
Scott and Pat Nyberg
Chris and Helen Roland
Colleen Ryan
Douglas and Bonnie Yingst

CONTENTS

THE INVISIBLE MADE VISIBLE

Location, location, location—the old saw about the basis of real estate value applies just as much to the value of what architect David Salmela has achieved in his small office in Duluth, Minnesota. He remains a widely recognized and highly regarded architect internationally, having won twenty-one AIA Minnesota honor awards, twenty-seven national awards, and an AIA Minnesota Gold Medal, with twenty-five of his projects having appeared in books and magazines around the world. Yet, he also has a deep affection for the Upper Midwest location of most of his work. "Thinking globally and acting locally applies to architectural practice," he observes. "Design is about making great things happen in any situation, regardless of the constraints."

Upper Midwest culture also holds a particular fascination for him. Of Finnish American descent, Salmela seems to understand well the cultures of northern climates. "I am not trying to be an American architect of Scandinavian descent," he says, "but our cultural roots come through in what we do." That applies to his clients as much as to himself. "My first meeting with clients is an important session. We talk a lot, getting to know each other. Many people won't disclose important things, so you have to extract it over time with questions," something that he has found especially true in northern Minnesota and Wisconsin, where, in his estimation, people are more restrained, frugal, and polite.

That sensibility pervades Salmela's view of architecture. For him, design involves simplifying, reducing, and distilling things down. And it affects his view of life. We are, he says, "affected by the remoteness of this place, more attuned to nature, and more reserved than in other parts of the country." At the same time, people don't hesitate to help each other, perhaps because of the harsh winters. He observes that the culture here is more about getting along than getting your own. The attitude that in sacrificing to make everyone healthy, we are all rewarded is as central to Salmela's progressive architecture as it is to the progressive politics of his region.

The vernacular architecture of the places in which Salmela builds also affects his work. "Vernacular architecture is about how to do things more efficiently," he says. "In Scandinavia, they built classical architecture out of wood, which was a fraction of the cost of the stone that the rest of Europe used." Such buildings "could be exuberant and expressive," he adds, "but they were also frugal." Fatalism can accompany that frugality, at least among the Finnish. "Finns all know architecture and music, and take cultural pride in buildings, but there is a fatalistic side to that self-confidence, convinced that others won't like it." After a pause, Salmela adds, "I have that same combination of confidence and insecurity."

Refreshingly so. When Salmela heard that he would receive AIA Minnesota's Gold Medal, he was shocked. "It was not something I expected or ever had as a goal," he says with characteristic modesty. "My mother used to say, 'Never think that you are better than someone else or eventually they'll be better than you.' " If such awards don't go to Salmela's head, neither do they lead him to want to rest on his laurels. "I think of the Gold Medal going to architects at the end of their careers, although I know that isn't always the case. I feel I'm just starting to learn things!"

Learning is something Salmela pursues with great passion. His library of architecture books and magazines from around the world, as well as his knowledge of the international architectural scene, all reflect his insatiable curiosity, borne of his being largely self-taught. "I haven't done things the way most architects do," he admits. Salmela did not go to architecture school, have a mentor, or work for big firms, and he did not live where most architects live. Instead, he worked in a couple of firms in northern Minnesota, became licensed before that required having an architectural degree, and has had a successful practice for many years.

The awards have gone to his buildings, but the rewards of his work often come from the interactions he has with his clients. "I had one client—two very successful professionals—say to me that the design and construction of their house was the most important thing they had ever done. It wasn't anything I did, in particular, but the very process transforms people." Contrary to the view that architecture is only for the rich and powerful, Salmela has made that process available to people of all sorts, in projects as small as stand-alone saunas. He believes that architecture can be created anyplace and that anyone can be involved in the process. What matters, he says, is having the right attitude: that we can make everyday life more memorable and more enjoyable through good design.

Salmela came to those insights gradually. "When I was younger," he says, "I wanted to do work that was up-to-date, but it wasn't well liked on the Iron Range, so I stepped back and asked myself what I should be doing. I realized that I needed to understand the immediate culture I was working in, while still trying to be progressive." That led Salmela on a path that has been so successful for him, with buildings that often look familiar, even nostalgic, at first glance, but that are really ultramodern and quite daring in their space and detail, frequently for very pragmatic reasons.

Salmela says that when he looked at ways to reduce costs and adjusted to the loss of craft skills among builders, he realized that he could build modern houses with flat roofs better and cheaper than traditional houses. He adds, with a laugh, that "those modern architects in the 1930s were really on to something!" And yet, unlike the early modernists, Salmela has managed to make modernism not only acceptable but also desirable for a wide range of his mostly residential clients. "The work draws people," he says. "Almost all of my clients are people I had never met before." The nostalgic first impression of his buildings plays a part in that. "As human beings, we can't avoid nostalgia," he says. "I'm nostalgic about early modern architecture."

He has been more than nostalgic. In his close working relationship with a couple of contractors for most of his projects, Salmela reminds us of the modernist goal of integrating design and construction. "Design-build allows you to reduce the amount and timeliness of drawings," he says. "When you work with the same builders, you understand their capabilities and they understand your expectations, so that you don't have to draw everything, resolving problems on the job site." Long working relationships between architects and contractors also lead to mutual respect. "My first question to my contractors is, 'What would you do?' I always respect the contractor's opinion."

Salmela shows the same respect for his staff. As staff members have moved, Salmela has retained them as employees, creating a "virtual" office as a result, with one architect working with him in Duluth, one working out of her home in Fargo, and his daughter and son-in-law, who are based in the Twin Cities. Digital technology has allowed that distribution of work, aided by cell phones that enable Salmela to stay in constant touch with his staff across such distances. But under it all lies his loyalty to people. He emphasizes that this form of practice arose out of necessity, from the desire to adapt to the movements of his staff. "Like working with the same contractors," he says, "keeping the same staff makes everything easier. I know what they can do and they know what I would do."

This follows the principle Salmela applies to clients and contractors: "Avoid difficult relationships if possible," he says. "That's why I don't do much public work. You have to be more hardnosed, which creates animosity with contractors, who, because they are the low bidders, are often looking for things you missed." Private work is different. "Clients come to you because they want to work with you. And if a contractor questions something, it's an opportunity to look at it again and make it better, which is easier on private jobs."

Having good relationships with clients and contractors also keeps costs down. Brad Holmes, who builds many of Salmela's projects, does early estimates after schematic design and late estimates after contract documents, producing a signed construction estimate with an itemized list. "Clients who want an absolute price end up paying more," Salmela explains, "because contractors need to cover the unknown on a fixed bid. If you use estimates, contractors give you the honest cost, with extras becoming not a legal matter but more about a fair revision to the estimate. If something doesn't go well that is our fault, we can take care of it right away."

All these practices recall the mix of tradition and innovation that characterized early modern architecture. We tend to see the abstract form and flowing space of modern buildings as a dramatic break from the past, but as Salmela shows in his work, that new aesthetic remained connected to a very old ethic that valued less formal and more natural ways of being. You see this in Salmela's close connections to his clients and contractors, in the familial way in which he treats his coworkers, and in the respect he shows for the natural world. "Things have to become more sustainable," observes Salmela. "We won't have a choice."

At first glance, Salmela's buildings don't look overtly "green," but you soon see how much they reflect his view of what a more sustainable future might be like. He can tick off its traits: minimal maintenance, minimal infrastructure, multiple uses of space, recycled materials, cross ventilation, passive solar heating, minimal air-conditioning, super insulation, high-quality windows and doors, and durable finishes. And it goes beyond materials and mechanical systems to the form of buildings. He believes the simplicity of the box is a sustainability strategy, as well as a cost-saving one.

These techniques may seem novel, but they are not. For most of human history, architecture employed these principles, making sustainability more a matter of remembering than of radical reform. Its only radical aspect stems from its resistance to the truly radical damage that has resulted from the mindless exploitation of nature over the past two centuries. A neighbor of Salmela, Ryan Vine, a professor of English at nearby College of St. Scholastica in Duluth, seemed to understand this when, in response to his passing the Clure development every day, he sent the architect this Wallace Stevens poem:

Anecdote of Men by the Thousand

The soul, he said, is composed
Of the external world.

There are men of the East, he said,
Who are the east.
There are men of a province
Who are that province.
There are men of a valley
Who are that valley.

There are men whose words
Are as natural sounds
Of their places
As the cackle of toucans
In the place of toucans.

The mandolin is the instrument
Of a place.

Are there mandolins of western mountains?
Are there mandolins of northern moonlight?

The dress of a woman of Lhassa,
In its place,
Is an invisible element of that place
Made visible.

Stevens's poetry, like Salmela's architecture, captures the sense of connection that modernism has long had with the distant past. The best modern work expresses the deep continuity that we all have, whether aware of it or not, with the cultures, climates, and contexts that we inhabit. Whether a poem or a building, a dress or a mandolin, such things make visible an invisible element of a place. This, in turn, suggests that we have probably put too much emphasis on the originality of modernism, focusing too much on how the artistic production of the twentieth century differs from what preceded it and not enough on how it has represented a new way of helping us recall what is most vital from the past and see what is least apparent about a place.

"Great architecture," says David Salmela, "makes you want to return to it, again and again, unable to explain what makes it so compelling, and yet amazed by the elusiveness and mystery of it all." Salmela is far too modest to call his own architecture great, but there is no question that his work rewards our returning to it over and over. And while we may ultimately be unable to explain what makes his designs so arresting, you will be amazed, as I have been, by the elusiveness and mystery of it all.

BOXES

FATHER AND SON

The average American household does not match the myth. According to the U.S. Census Bureau, only 32 percent of households consist of married couples with children, a number that is only slightly ahead of the households of married couples without children (28 percent) and single people living alone (26 percent). Meanwhile the number of households headed by a male grew 44 percent in just an eight-year period between 1995 and 2003 and now constitutes 2 percent of all families. The home-building industry has adjusted to these demographic changes slowly, at best. Most of the mass-market homes available in many locations assume larger families, able to do more maintenance and needing more room than these statistics suggest.

Recent demographic shifts have in turn created a great need for more adaptable, compact, and diverse housing types than currently exist. Although many buyers think they cannot afford a custom-designed home, they typically end up buying more house than they need and one that doesn't necessarily fit their family's lifestyle. This decision can be less cost effective than hiring an architect and a custom builder to design and construct a house that meets their requirements without wasted space or expense.

The house and surrounding site that architect David Salmela and landscape architect Shane Coen designed for Kevin Streeter and his son demonstrate the advisability of the custom-built route. They show how the dramatic increase in the number of male-headed households has begun to affect the size and nature of housing, and indicates the extent to which creative new models can arise when offering people real choices in the home market. A builder of custom homes himself, Streeter admits that "there are a lot of terrible houses being built these days."

From the road, the Streeter house looks uncanny, with its two white boxes on a black base reflected in the water of the wetland in front of it.

There certainly are not many designed specifically for single-father households. "I'm passionate about unique houses," he adds, "which I often can't do for clients. A lot of people aren't brave enough to build a house like this, so I had to do it myself."

Having built six previous houses for himself, Streeter discovered David Salmela's work through a mutual friend, the photographer Peter Bastianelli-Kerze. "David is very perceptive," says Streeter. "He picks up quickly what a client and a site need, and I completely trusted him. It worked well." Salmela says much the same about Streeter. "Kevin was very involved in the development of the house. We talked about it all the time." The resulting structure, winner of several design awards, reflects that mutually supportive relationship and represents its father and son occupants in several ways.

Most notable are the two white bedroom boxes that sit on top of a black-painted masonry base containing the rest of the house. With their blank side walls and wood-slat screens on their end walls, those two boxes, one slightly smaller than the other, echo the house's two inhabitants: biologically linked and similar in appearance, and yet separate individuals, each with his own private life to lead.

To hear David Salmela describe the house, the design was almost inevitable. "Kevin had a very restrictive lot," says Salmela, "with one brother living next door and another across the pond. Once we worked out the logic of bringing a car into the site, without having a garage next to the entrance, it led to the creation of an auto court, which determined where the rest of the house had to go. The small footprint also led us to put some of the house above the rest."

The way in which you approach and enter the house, however, and the way in which the spaces lay out inside were anything but inevitable. Almost every aspect of the design seems suited to how a father and son would want to live. Forget the grand entrance and impressive foyer that have become clichés in high-end homes. Here, you walk along the front wall of the house and enter through a glass door under the overhang of one of the boxes, a simple and unpretentious way of getting in. And don't bother with formalities like sitting rooms with settees. Here, the entire main floor of the house occupies a single, expansive space, with living and dining areas facing the pond, kitchen and laundry areas along the back wall, and a screened porch facing the adjacent public trail. "There are only two interior doors in the house," notes Salmela, "one on the powder room and the other between the house and the garage."

opposite: The wood-framed screened porch, with its black masonry chimney, has its own paved terrace, shielded by a masonry wall from the nearby bike path.

above: The two bedroom boxes, which project out over the masonry living areas, have wood-slat end walls that let in light while providing visual privacy.

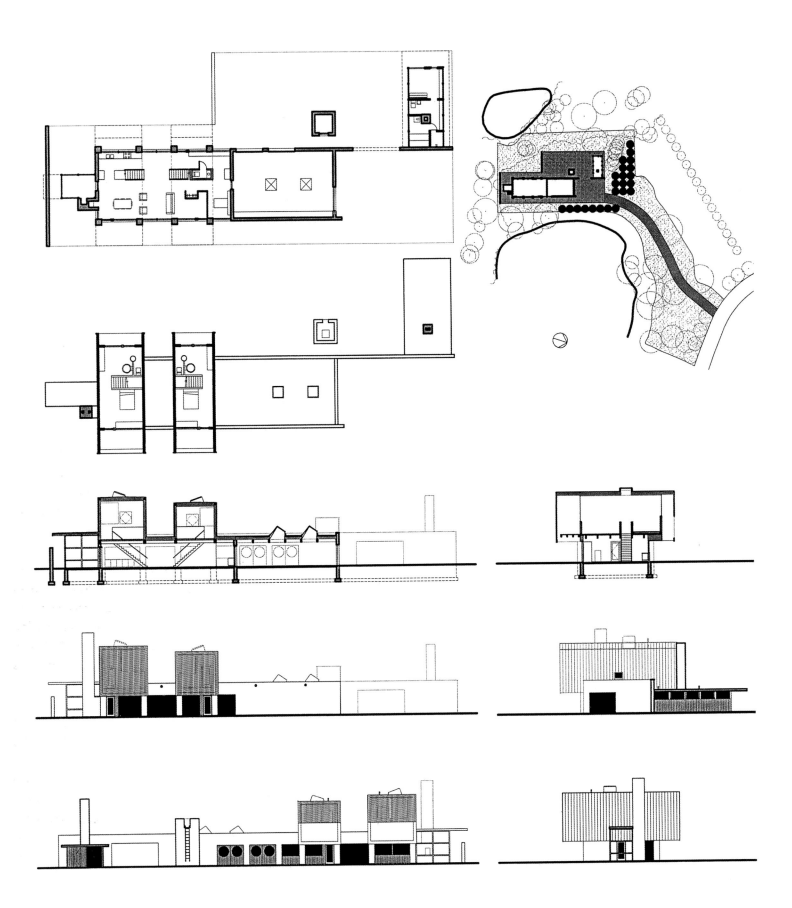

opposite: The plans, elevations, and sections of the Streeter house seem deceptively simple given the spatial complexity and visual richness of the place.

right: This approach to the house features a paved parking area and a walk that leads under the projecting white boxes to the front door.

And what a garage it is. Taking up almost half of the house's main level, the garage contains ample space for the owner's motorcycles, with a wall of equipment and tool storage, a picture window facing the entrance drive, and two garage doors whose double portal windows echo the headlights of the bikes inside. It's a big playroom for the mechanical machinations of American male culture.

The two bedrooms exhibit another side of that culture. Accessed by opposed straight-run stairs encased in white wood slats, the bedroom boxes have the same plans, with a large, open bathroom on one side of the stairwell and a sleeping area on the other side, lit by large, glass end walls. A porch, screened from the street by full-height wood slats, offers each bedroom an amazingly peaceful, Zen-like space that speaks to the more sensitive and sedate side of the American male.

For those times when father and son need some space, Salmela has designed a separate sauna and guesthouse that runs perpendicular to the main building and encloses one side of the rear auto court. That sense of enclosure, combined with the mechanical room's chimney, which rises above the paved court like a campanile, creates an outdoor plaza that feels remarkably urban, in the middle of the woods. Those options of places to be in and around the house make a very compact structure, by most home-building standards, feel much larger and, more important, more private than it otherwise might.

In what some consider the first modern Russian novel, *Fathers and Sons,* Ivan Turgenev wrote about the conflicts that can arise between males of different generations in a family. Some 150 years later, Salmela has given us one of the first houses of the twenty-first century that shows how architecture can temper the tensions that naturally occur between father and son, providing a place in which the two generations can come together and also be apart. And rarely has residential architecture taken up such an issue in such a simple and straightforward way as the Streeter house. "David likes to do the unexpected," says Streeter. "I've never lived in a house this comfortable," he adds. "I can be home all day and never feel the need to go out." And that, says Salmela, "is the greatest compliment any client can give."

above: Almost elemental in its simplicity, the screened porch has a projecting roof that hovers above the terrace, while reaching out to what lies beyond the wall.

right: A wood bench beside the front door provides a sheltered place to look out on the landscape and to take off boots before entering the house.

An identical wood bench in the entry vestibule offers a place to sit or unload packages before moving into the adjacent living and dining areas.

above: The two stairs leading to the father's and son's bed-rooms frame the living room, which has a full-height glass wall overlooking the wetland.

opposite, top: Enclosed in white slats, the stairs seem to glow with light, in contrast to the dark masonry of the dining room fireplace and the polished concrete floor.

opposite, bottom, left: In the bedrooms, the stair enclosure separates the open bathroom from the sleeping area, each illuminated by high windows and low-voltage lighting.

opposite, bottom, middle: The wood floor casts a warm glow in the bedroom and bathroom, whose white walls and ceiling echo the white slats that provide privacy over the windows.

opposite, bottom, right: Each bedroom has an exterior deck, open to the air but enclosed with white slats that give ethe-real light and offer glimpses of the landscape.

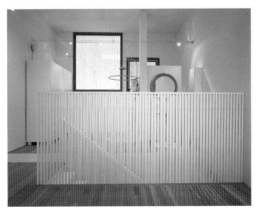

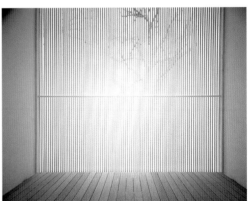

top: The rear auto court has a wood-clad sauna building on one side and a mechanical-room tower that separates the entry drive from the garage.

bottom: Seen from the backyard, the Streeter house offers an elegant composition of white and black forms offset by infill elements of natural wood.

top: The garage, with its wall of white storage closets, provides a well-lit space for the owner's motorcycles, whose round headlamps are echoed in the doors.

bottom: Visually as well as thermally warm, the sauna has beautifully crafted wood benches, sidewalls, and ceiling, in contrast to the black masonry end wall.

AS GREEN AS IT GETS

We hear a lot about the "green economy" without always knowing what it means. For some, it implies an economy that uses environmentally friendly methods of making and delivering the products and services we have today, while for others it suggests something more dramatic: a complete change in the relationship between humans and the natural environment, resulting in new kinds of products and services and in the cessation of the most damaging things we do right now. These two views—one more evolutionary, the other more revolutionary—do not necessarily exclude each other. We can evolve more slowly in areas that do not have much effect on the environment as long as we move quickly in those that do. What matters is how fast we expand what we mean by the bottom line, determining profit not only in financial terms but also in consideration of the benefits our actions have on others—other people, other species, other generations.

That may not sound like a formula for economic success, but green companies have begun to prove skeptics wrong. Businesses that value people and the planet as much as conventional ideas about profit have done very well, as exemplified in two companies, Loll and Epicurean, whose owners commissioned David Salmela to design their offices and production facility in a renovated industrial building in Duluth. "They are young, progressive companies," says Salmela, "with innovative, sustainability-minded products," and their success shows that business owners can care about their employees, attend to the natural environment, and produce eco-friendly products while also building economic value.

The companies started as a design-build firm, making TrueRide skateboard parks. The surface they used consisted of a paper-based, fiber-composite material—Skatelite—that resisted the

wear and tear of skateboarders to a remarkable degree. The firm also used postconsumer high-density polyethylene derived from recycled plastic containers to make the substructure supporting the skateboard surface. Eventually, brothers Dave Benson and Greg Benson, along with Tony Ciardelli, began using the scrap from making skateboard parks to manufacture Loll Designs outdoor furniture and Epicurean cutting boards, all made from recycled materials. "We're a little different from other companies," admits Greg Benson, and when it came to expanding their facilities, "we didn't want something traditional."

In industry, "traditional" usually means building a new structure from scratch, often using high-energy materials in locations that require a lot of fossil-fueled transportation. Instead, Benson and his two co-owners bought an eighty-year-old factory in the city of Duluth, next to a train line, with the goal of recycling it, in the spirit of their products. The factory, called Hawks Boots, had had several additions over the years, with a manufacturer of concrete burial vaults having occupied it last, leaving behind contaminated soil, cement waste, and concrete debris, which the new owners cleaned up with the oversight of the Minnesota Pollution Control Agency. And yet, despite the expense of this cleanup, the building offered great value, with high-ceilinged production spaces and a spectacular view from its easily accessible roof, of the St. Louis River and Duluth's harbor in the distance.

The building lacked adequate office space, however, and so Benson and his co-owners approached David Salmela. "We knew about David's buildings, such as his Gooseberry Falls State Park Visitors Center," says Benson, "and we knew he could give us something comfortable to work in." That Salmela had worked on an industrial building earlier in his career was also a plus. What cemented the relationship was Salmela's seeing the potential of the fiber-composite board that the company uses in its cutting boards as a possible cladding material for the building. "We realized in the first fifteen minutes that they had an amazing product," says Salmela. Skatelite can withstand severe weather and it has an integral color that needs no painting and little maintenance. Its use in the company's offices would serve as an ideal advertisement for the durability of the company's sustainable products. "David liked the slate-black color the best, which also has the best performance for the exterior of buildings," adds Benson, "because it fades the least."

Salmela and Benson realized that the factory's roof provided the best place for the five-thousand-square-foot addition. That location not only offered "an amazing view," says Salmela, it also separated the offices from the manufacturing below and provided an easy entry point on the uphill side of the site. Using the concrete debris on the property, Salmela created two grass-covered earth berms that flank the entrance to the offices and guide visitors to the wood-slat enclosure that covers the stairs to the front door of the addition. They also provide some visual separation between the offices and parking area. "The berms are like the mounds that Martha Schwartz uses in her landscapes," jokes Salmela, "but here they serve an environmental purpose, keeping waste material out of the landfill."

The project's modest budget—sixty-three dollars per square foot, including site work and demolition—demanded that the addition be, as Salmela says, "a simple, bold, modern space made of inexpensive materials." The rooftop addition consists of one large, sixteen-foot-high room, with full-height glass walls on either end and exposed glulam columns and beams running the length of the space. Structural-insulated panels make up the walls and roof, with the company's slate-black material cladding both the interior and exterior walls, contrasting beautifully with the exposed wood structure and the plywood floor stained a red-and-white checkerboard pattern. Salmela's office also designed the cubicle system for the client, using the same recycled polyethylene material they use in their outdoor furniture. "It showed off what their products can do," says Salmela, "and let them avoid having to order new furniture."

The office interior features a checkerboard painted floor, wood beams and ceiling, large windows and skylights, and black Skatelite sidewalls.

A wide, daylighted stair connects the office to a mezzanine lounge area to which all the employees have access. Down an additional stair, you come to the manufacturing floor, where computer-controlled machines laser-cut the products from the recycled boards, with scrap material captured and sorted for reuse. Salmela helped the company lay out its production and assembly areas, with a wide corridor connecting the various areas and glass garage doors creating a well-lit and easily navigated facility. "It's an incredible space to work in," says Benson. "When it snows, it feels like you are in one of those glass snow globes." And when you visit the factory, you begin to get a sense of what the green economy might look like: generous in its accommodation of people, responsible in its treatment of the environment, and creative in its reuse of materials. "Business is a constant process of simplifying procedures, reducing waste, improving quality, and lowering cost," observes Benson. The same could be said about design, as David Salmela has demonstrated so clearly here.

above, top: Enclosed in horizontal wood slats, the metal entry stair is a sheltered space for people entering or leaving the light-filled addition.

above, bottom: The open porch at the end of the office offers a distant view of Duluth, with the company's Loll outdoor furniture providing places to sit.

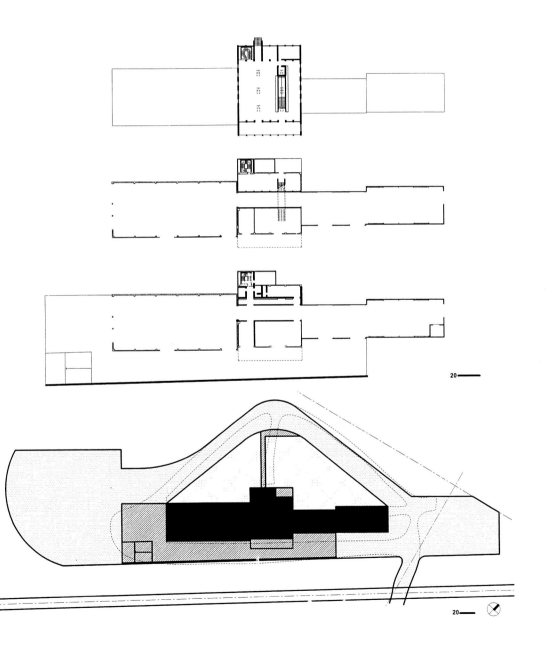

left: Glulam beams extend from the front of the office to the back, supported by glulam columns stiffened with steel X-bracing inside the glass.

above: The conference room, with its white light fixtures hanging from the ceiling, looks out to the entrance enclosure and wooded hillside beyond.

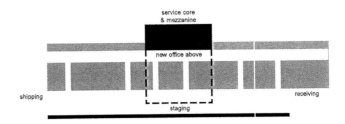

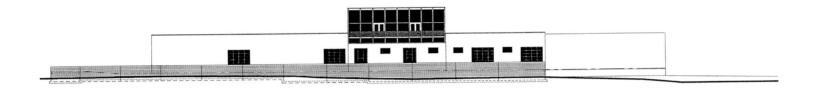

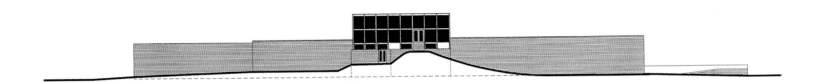

10 ——

Placing the office on top of the existing factory required
structural reinforcement of the original factory to handle the
extra weight of the new building.

CHRISMER CABIN

ELLISON BAY, WISCONSIN

THE ZEN OF NATURE

This is the forest primeval. The murmuring pines and hemlocks,
Bearded with moss, and in garments green, indistinct in the twilight,
Stand like Druids of eld, with voices sad and prophetic
—from "Evangeline," by Henry Wadsworth Longfellow

When Bob and Alice Chrismer purchased their wooded site in Wisconsin's Door County, it reminded Alice of a poem she read when a child. In "Evangeline," Longfellow gives "the forest primeval" as much a part to play in the story as the human protagonists. He assigns the "pines and hemlocks" personalities, "bearded with moss, and in garments green," and casts them in the role of stoic "Druids" observing the joys and sorrows of Evangeline as she finds, loses, and ultimately rediscovers her true love, Gabriel.

We moderns might mock such romantic sentiments. Our more matter-of-fact approach leads us to view the forest analytically, as a functioning ecology rather than a murmuring stand of Druids. Still, Alice immediately sensed something primeval in the land they had purchased and in the forest where they would build their house. She had seen in a publication the home and studio that David Salmela had created for Jim Brandenburg, and she wanted Salmela to design a cabin for her and her husband to accommodate them on weekends and eventually full-time, with space for their grown children to visit.

"Initially, David told us he was too busy," says Bob Chrismer, "but we were persistent and when he saw the property, he got excited about the project." The personality of the pines and

hemlocks came through. Salmela set the house into the sloping site, with a stone retaining wall—that Bob Chrismer built—defining a flat, rectangular piece of ground on which the house could stand. "Setting it down like that," observes Bob Chrismer, "increased our privacy from the road." Or, as Salmela describes it, "The cabin is like a small, woodland animal lying low among the trees," an analogy that Longfellow would have appreciated.

According to the local zoning laws, however, the structure couldn't be too small, which led to a design in which three elements initially thought of as distinct—the sauna, the guest area, and the main cabin—became linked into a single ensemble. A long flat roof extends beyond the main house to cover the sauna and its adjoining bathroom and mechanical room, creating an entrance breezeway, lit by a central skylight and furnished with a long bench for taking off and putting on outdoor gear. Meanwhile the guest space, which doubles as a family room and study, sits on top of the other end of the flat roof, as a wood-clad box supported on two stout white columns, looking like an animal about to spring into action.

Inside the front door and past the line of closets and the large bathroom on the left, the cabin opens up into one large room. The master bedroom has a sliding door and a wood-clad partition that visually separate it from the main living areas, while allowing the long, low ceiling to extend uninterrupted over the otherwise private space. Walls of wood-framed windows on both sides

of the house flood it with light and reinforce the continuity of the single room, within which furniture and other objects sit. Two elements do the most to organize the space. A white masonry fireplace separates the living area from the hallway and provides a focal point for the classic modern furniture the Chrismers have collected, while the kitchen island, which contains the sink, cooktop, oven, dishwasher, and under-the-counter refrigerator, divides the dining area from the space for food preparation. "It's all very Zen-like," says Alice Chrismer, "with not a lot of distractions."

As a religious practice, Zen stresses our enlightenment through a sense of oneness with nature, and the Chrismers' house certainly fulfills that principle. A large opening in the ceiling above the kitchen not only connects the first-floor living spaces with the guest room and study above but also floods the center of house with light from a doubly pitched skylight overhead. A light fixture suspended from the second-floor ceiling all the way down to the first-floor kitchen reinforces the sense of that opening, surrounded by shimmering wood-slat railings and walls, as a source of illumination.

The forest, ever present in the cabin because of full-height windows, takes on a particularly mysterious, Zen-like quality in the dining area. There, two enormous windows rise up from the level of the Salmela-designed table, past the ceiling, to illuminate the second floor, up to the height of the built-in table in the study above. That shared pair of windows has two very different effects. On the first floor, it draws your attention up into the trees, emphasizing their height and age, "bearded with moss" as Longfellow put it. And on the second level, the windows along the floor focus your view down to the forest floor, "indistinct in the twilight" of deep shade.

Modern design is often associated with machine production and mechanical forms, but the Scandinavian version of modernism has often sought, instead, to reconnect us to nature by opening up buildings to their surroundings and by using natural materials. You see that sentiment in Salmela's use of wood, left in its natural state, on both the inside and outside of houses such as the Chrismers'. And you also see it in what Salmela's clients often select as furnishings. In the Chrismers' case, long before they commissioned Salmela to design their house, they had purchased a number of vintage Danish modern chairs by the well-known designer Børge Mogensen. Made of undyed leather strapping slung over clear-finished wood

above: From the road, the Chrismer cabin lies low to the ground. Only the white line of the roof, the white chimney, and the wood-clad box are clearly visible.

opposite, top: At dusk, the cabin glows from within as light bounces off the wood cladding, the white walls, the wood windows, and warm gray concrete floors.

opposite, bottom: The entry hall leads along the window wall, past the living room fireplace, to end in the dining area and kitchen, which is open to the floor above.

The white masonry fireplace is a focal point in the living room, with views past it to the woods or to the wood-slat balcony over the kitchen.

frames, the Mogensen furniture provides the seating in the dining and living areas, and "it goes perfectly with David's design," observed Bob Chrismer. Having first bought the chairs, adds Alice Chrismer, with a smile, "we had to have David design a home for them."

Sometimes, of course, we don't recognize the inevitability of things. "The one thing we fought David on were the four-foot-wide white overhangs on the roof," admits Bob Chrismer. "We thought they would look out-of-place with the dark color of the house and would block our view of the trees, but David insisted on them, and he was right. They're wonderful." As in Longfellow's poem, where it seems unavoidable that Evangeline will one day reunite with Gabriel, so too does the simplicity of the Chrismers' cabin seem effortless, as natural as the murmuring pines that surround it.

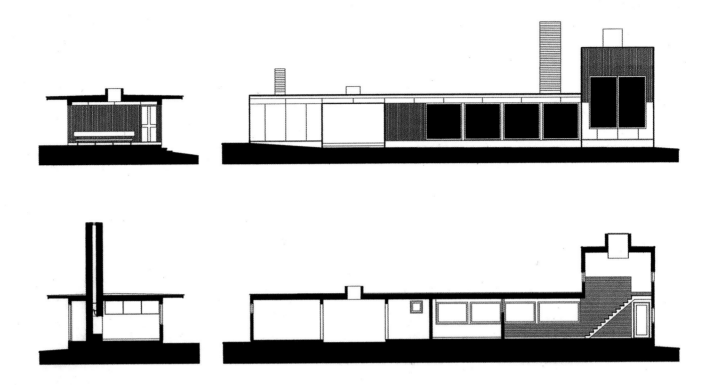

above: A sauna and mechanical room create a breezeway, with an entry hall that leads past a bathroom and master bedroom to the living spaces beyond.

opposite: A skylight illuminates the upstairs spaces as well as the kitchen below, visually warming the volume as light bounces off the wood surfaces.

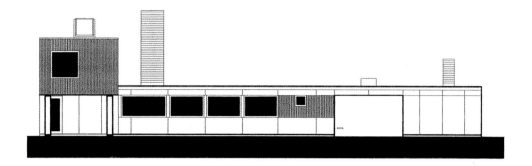

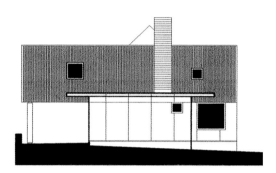

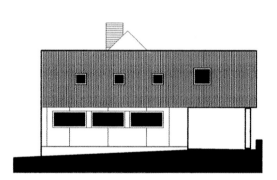

opposite: The study upstairs shares the two-story window with the dining room below, as well as receiving borrowed light from the skylight over the kitchen.

this page: The cabin stands behind a low retaining wall, built into the hillside, that creates privacy from the road and a flat site in the sloping forest floor.

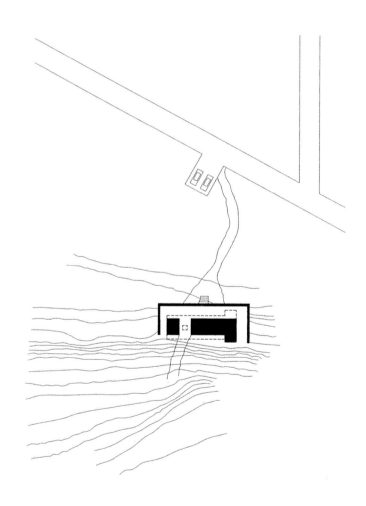

ARTIST LOFTS

Artist lofts tell us as much about ourselves as they do about the place of artists in our society. Artists have long sought out low-rent quarters to make ends meet and to have suitable space in which to work. Where that once often meant occupying garret apartments, it came to mean, in the twentieth century, inhabiting industrial spaces that manufacturers had abandoned as they moved production lines to the suburbs or other less expensive locations. Along with loft living arose a certain aesthetic—a mix of minimal furniture, ample open space, high ceilings, and a lot of light—that echoed the minimalist and abstract nature of much of the art produced there, and reflected values of creativity and individuality that have come to define the modern person as much as the modern artist.

These factors set up the somewhat paradoxical situation in which the low-cost accommodations of artists who had little choice but to live that way became the high-end lifestyle of those who could afford to live in other ways, but who liked what lofts said about their values and them. Artists and their patrons still often live far apart, since real estate values have yet to catch up with modern egalitarian values. But the spaces in which the production and consumption of art occur have become remarkably similar, reversing centuries of difference in the way artists and patrons lived. Lofts have come to embody emancipation from the expectations of others and from ourselves.

Rarely have those two worlds come together as clearly as in the retreat David Salmela has designed for Mike Ryan, a financial adviser, and his wife, Pam, an artist. Located on a five-hundred-acre site, with its own lake, this retreat for a couple from Chicago "ended up becoming a

Overlooking its own artificial lake, the Ryan retreat stands on a rocky promontory with slots cut into the line of trees to provide views of the water.

compound," says Salmela. The Ryans initially had a neighbor build a small timber-framed house on a high point on the site near the lake, but "we loved David's design for Wild Rice restaurant," said Mike Ryan, "and decided to hire him to design the garage that we had already bought the timber for." "The first time I visited the site," adds Salmela, "I realized that they needed something in front of the existing cabin, and so I designed a tall, stand-alone screened porch that looks like a giant window announcing that you have arrived. It was the first thing I designed and the last thing built."

Salmela also designed the garage the Ryans wanted, using standard wood framing, rather than the timber frames already purchased, to create a long shed roof structure whose clerestory of translucent glazing floods the interior of the garage with an even light, filtered through the trusses. Seeing that plan, the Ryans decided to commission Salmela to design a house and sauna for them on the site, turning the existing cabin into a guesthouse.

"The land was very overgrown," says Salmela, "but when we discovered the rock ledge above the lake, we knew we had the right location for the new house." Once they cleared some of the trees and underbrush and saw the large amount of pink-and-gray granite, that rock became a colorful anchor for the whole project, a substantial, sculptural object that you walk beside on your way to the house.

Although far from the art world of Chicago, the house embodies the double meaning of the loft in almost every aspect of its design. A long structure, running parallel to the lake, contains the living and sleeping spaces under a high shed roof that opens up to the south and affords a view of the water. Low partitions separate the various areas of the loftlike house, with repetitive structural-timber columns and a tall wood-clad ceiling that continues, uninterrupted, from one end to the other. On top of that structure, at the entry end of the house, stands Pam Ryan's painting studio in the form of a tall, black-clad box, with glass walls at either end. Whereas in a city those two realms, the loft for living in and the loft for working in, would likely not occur in the same place, here they join into a single composition, with painter and patron one above the other.

above: The side of the house shows how it stands on top of a concrete podium, with a black-clad box hovering above a wood-framed screened porch.

right: From the bottom of the hill, the house reflects the sky in its glass walls, its white roof edge, and the deep blue of its exterior walls.

In many ways Pam Ryan's second-floor loft represents the kind of place that all painters want. Its spare white interior, with a substantial easel in the center of the room; its large windows facing south, east, and north; and its high ceiling and low cabinets for storing materials provide the space and light that artists have long needed to work. But rarely do we get to see, so directly, the impact of artists' environments on the way many people now like to live. That effect becomes clear almost the moment you step onto the concrete plinth that supports the Ryans' house. A low-ceiling entry area features a screened enclosure and a broad terrace and stair that look out over the surrounding countryside, as if to entice us not to enter the house itself, but to go and experience nature directly and decide for ourselves what we think, as so much art urges us to do.

When we finally do go inside, however, the house offers us two surprisingly informal ways of entering, with one door leading to a vestibule under the stair up to the loft and the other door leading directly into the kitchen. Both have the quality of back doors or service entrances, reflecting the informality that has characterized the lives of artists and come to define much of modern life. The kitchen and vestibule open up to a large living and dining space with classic modern furniture arranged like pieces of minimalist sculpture across the slate floor and in front of a white-painted masonry fireplace. The size and airiness of that light-filled room recall the abundance of square footage in former industrial lofts, while the quality of the furniture and solidity of materials also bring to mind a generous museum space that looks out, in this case, to nature rather than to the art inspired by it.

The rest of the house sits among wood-clad partitions, slightly above head height, that wind their way through the space. To the left of the fireplace stands a utility and washroom and to the right, a book-lined office—areas that would feel right at home in a working artist's loft. At the far end of the long room stands a bedroom, with a large closet area and toilet and bathtub enclosures divided by a common sink. Here, too, the quality of the bedroom, small by most standards, reflects that found in many artists' studios, where sleeping seems more like a distraction from the work in progress.

Indeed, there exists at the Ryans' compound a pull that occurs in most of our lives between working, whether in an office or a loft, and relaxing, as in the sauna and screened porch that beckon across the driveway. Even out in nature, hundreds of miles from our official workplaces, that tug remains with us, and it suggests that the real influence art has had on life amounts to more than the loft spaces that so many people now occupy. It has led to an inseparability of living and working that artists have long known and that technology has now made a fact of life for us all.

opposite: Like a large painting, the art loft stands above the wood-framed main house and screened porch as if propped on an easel.

above: A stand-alone, two-story screened porch offers a covered gathering place for the Ryans and their guests in the adjacent cabin.

left: The garage and screened porch, visible behind the rock ledge flanking the entrance path, were constructed before the house was built.

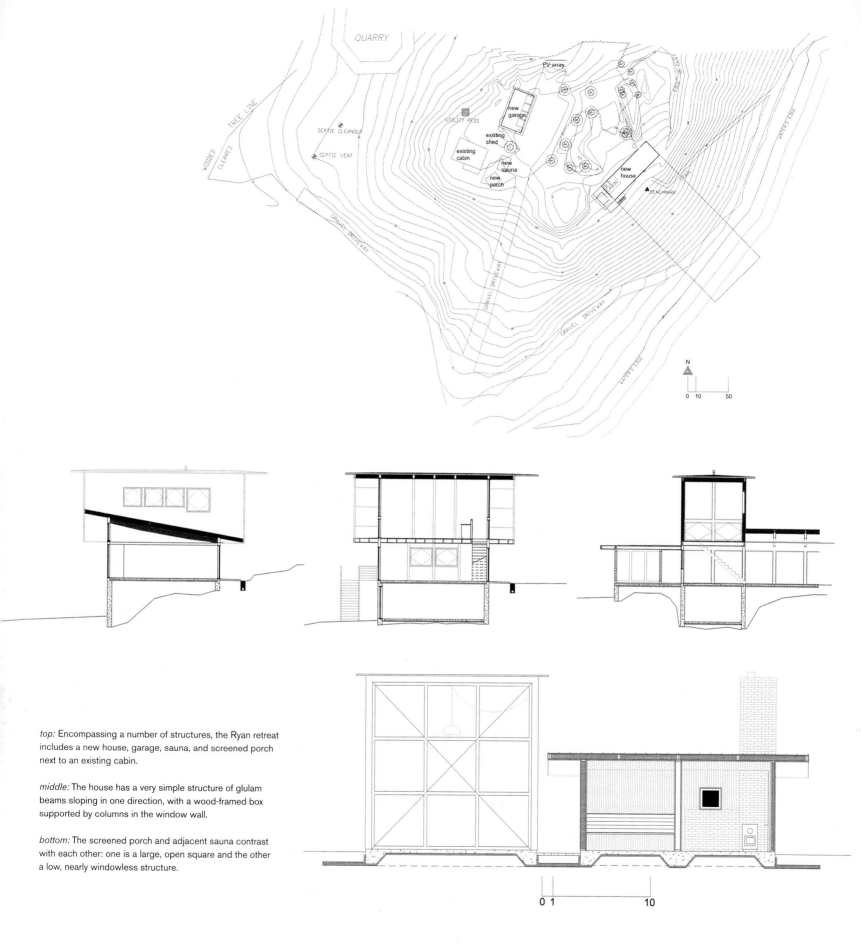

top: Encompassing a number of structures, the Ryan retreat includes a new house, garage, sauna, and screened porch next to an existing cabin.

middle: The house has a very simple structure of glulam beams sloping in one direction, with a wood-framed box supported by columns in the window wall.

bottom: The screened porch and adjacent sauna contrast with each other: one is a large, open square and the other a low, nearly windowless structure.

top: Red cabinets in the kitchen contrast with the natural wood finish of the windows and with the white walls, countertops, and ceiling.

bottom left: The sloped ceiling opens up to the light and view and emphasizes the single space of the living and sleeping areas, separated by low, wood-clad walls.

bottom right: Looking back through the open stair to the glass entry door, you can see the bottom of the black art loft providing a lower ceiling over the kitchen.

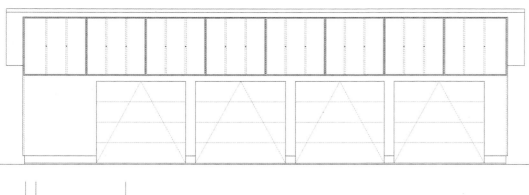

top: The interior of the loft provides a light-filled space and ample storage, ideal for the production of paintings and the enjoyment of views.

bottom: The four-bay garage has a sloped roof and translucent glazing above the garage doors that lets ample light into the interior.

0 1   10

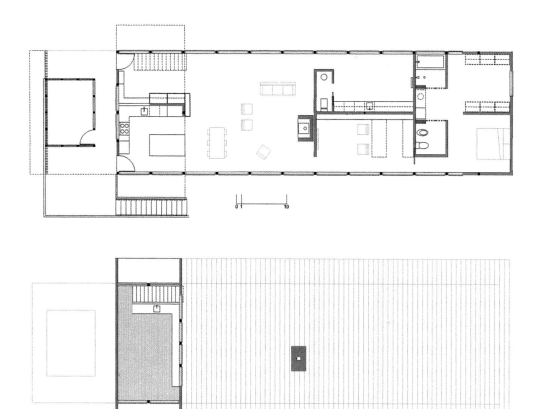

top: The main house has an entry vestibule and kitchen at one end and a master bedroom suite at the other, with living spaces and an office in between.

bottom: To take advantage of the gorgeous and secluded site, the house has walls of glass front and back and a nearly windowless side elevation.

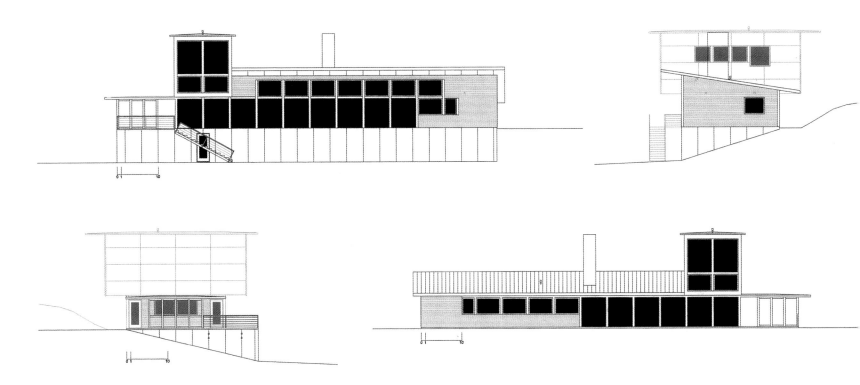

TRAILER TALK

Construction trailers exist on every job site, and yet, for all the attention given to buildings themselves, we rarely give any thought to the structures in which contractors work as they build. Kevin Streeter, whose house David Salmela designed and who has built several Salmela houses, wanted a job site trailer that would convey the quality of his construction company's work and reflect the attention Streeter and his staff give to everything they do. Salmela started with a stock flatbed frame, on which was built an insulated wood-framed structure with drywall interior walls and black Skatelite paper-resin panels as the exterior cladding. Perforated stainless steel panels cover the aluminum windows for security purposes, while recycled teak spacers behind the panels add an unexpected touch of warmth, echoing the vertical wood studs within. A perforated metal platform outside the door provides a comfortable way of entering the trailer. Inside, white built-in casework, a heated slate floor, and low-voltage lighting enhance the white-painted walls, providing a comfortable and classy place to work and meet amidst the messy conditions of job sites. "The job site trailer," writes Salmela, "is a neglected building type that this contractor hopes to raise to a new level." That he does, prompting the question of why all contractors can't have the same working conditions as those for whom they build.

opposite: Parked on construction sites like a portable piece of a Salmela building, the trailer conveys the quality that the Streeters seek in all they build.

top: The trailer is clad in black Skatelite panels, and its windows have white metal-mesh screens to protect them from damage.

bottom: Boot scrapers on the platform in front of the trailer's entrance keep mud out of the pristine interior of the trailer.

top: The spare, white interior of the trailer epitomizes the cleanliness and order that one can always hope for in a well-managed construction project.

bottom: Contrasting with the somewhat chaotic nature of a construction site, the trailer evinces the neatness and precision of a minimalist sculpture.

opposite: The construction trailer consists of a simple box, with windows on every side providing ample illumination of the desk and built-in storage.

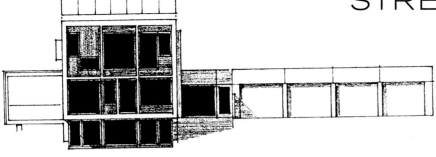

STREETER MODEL HOME

DEEPHAVEN, MINNESOTA

HYBRID HOUSE

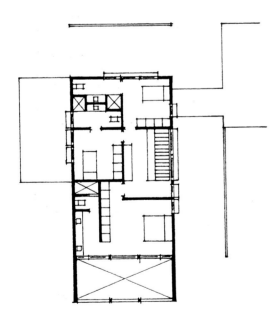

Hybrid cars have offered us a way of making big vehicles more efficient, and the same might be said of this model home that David Salmela designed for Streeter Associates on a plot of land near Kevin Streeter's own Salmela-designed house. Reacting to the costly complexity of so many large suburban houses built in recent years, Salmela set out to design a "compact house that has everything those larger houses have," he says. A driveway leads up to an auto court facing a flat-roofed, four-car garage, reflecting the car culture that propels so much suburban development. A glass entryway connects the garage to the house, a simple metal-clad rectangular structure that cantilevers out over the lot's south-facing slope, with a ten-foot-deep hood around the south-facing windows and projecting frames around the east- and west-facing openings. Inside, the main living level has a powder room, closets, and kitchen treated as an island floating in a single space, with access to a slat-enclosed deck extending to the west and a private terrace to the north. Upstairs, three bedrooms have ample closet space and their own bathrooms, gathered around a stair hall lit by a large, east-facing window, which also lights the lower level recreational room and bathroom sauna. "I wanted it to recall the expressive modernism of Ralph Rapson's architecture," says Salmela. It does.

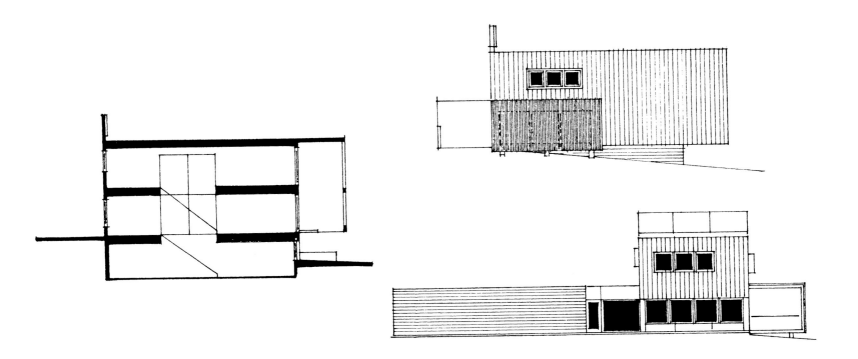

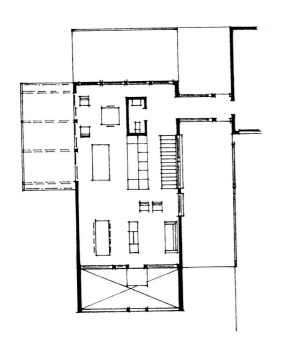

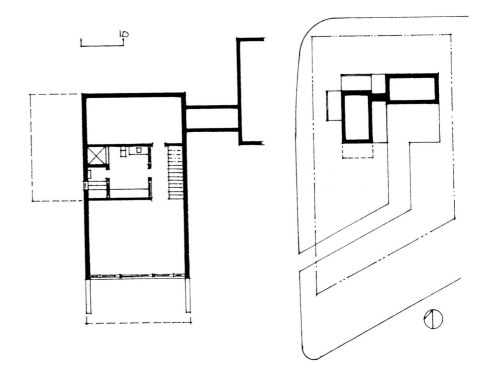

This model house packs a great deal of functional space
(three bedrooms and living and recreational rooms) into
a compact boxlike form.

BAGLEY NATURE PAVILION

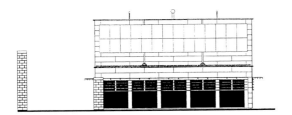

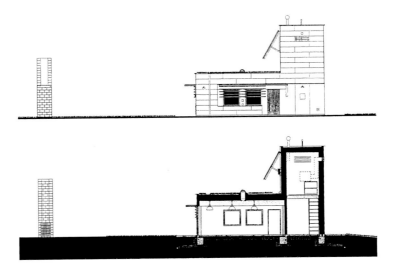

BACK TO NATURE

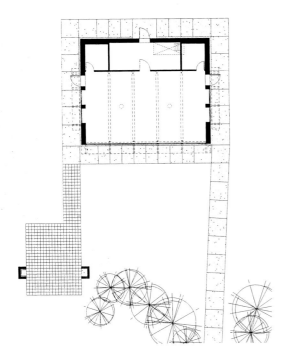

To maximize efficiency and minimize cost, the building has a very simple plan, with a large teaching space and mechanical and toilet rooms along the rear.

Universities, as the long-term owners of buildings, have an opportunity—and responsibility—to construct greener structures than the private sector might consider. David Salmela's design for the Bagley Nature Pavilion at the University of Minnesota, Duluth, shows how far universities can go to demonstrate the best of green building. Located in a clearing in the woods, overlooking Rock Pond on the campus, the educational center consists of a large single-story teaching space adjacent to a two-story service zone containing toilets, storage, and mechanical room. The simplicity of the structure has helped reduce its cost and ease construction; in fact, it was largely built by the university's facilities staff. But the building was designed for a LEED Platinum as well as a Passive House rating. "If those are achieved, it may be one of the first public buildings in the United States to be certified in both," speculates Salmela. Built with recycled timbers, the structure has sixteen-inch structural-insulated-panel walls and high-performance windows; oiled concrete floors and unfinished basswood finishes on its interior; recycled zinc and Skatelite panels on its exterior; recycled granite pavers and recycled wood benches in the landscape; and exterior louvered shades, a planted roof, and photovoltaic panels along the south elevation. "We wanted the building to be a learning facility," says Salmela. "It took an immense amount of time, but it will be worth it."

The nature center features an exterior chimney, a glass-walled classroom shaded by louvers, and a photovoltaic array along a mechanical penthouse.

KRAUSE CABIN

ALL IN THE FAMILY

opposite: Using the same Skatelite panels and wood windows, Salmela creates a great deal of continuity among the three buildings in this cabin compound.

The Krause family has owned land on Little Long Lake in Ely, Minnesota, for a long time, with a cabin on the site that needed to come down. With German and Finnish heritage and a lot of furniture by Alvar Aalto, the Krauses gravitated naturally to David Salmela to design a new cabin and guest cabin. A long, white masonry garage greets you as you come down the drive, shielding the house behind it. Clad in black Skatelite over a base of white Thorosealed masonry, the adjacent cabin has a front terrace with a low wall and corner outdoor fireplace that turns the south-facing space into an exterior room. You enter the cabin through a wide, glass-walled link that connects the bathroom, bedroom, and study wing with the single kitchen/dining/living room. Stairs lead down to a second bathroom and a television room with outdoor access, next to a deck whose wide stairs open out to the lake. Farther down the drive, you come upon the guest cabin, with a white masonry garage in front of a black Skatelite-clad two-story structure. Inside, a first-floor living space and second-story bedroom look out through large windows to the lake. A small kitchen unit and enclosed bathroom tuck under a sleeping loft above. "It's a nearly maintenance-free retreat," says Salmela, and it's still all in the family.

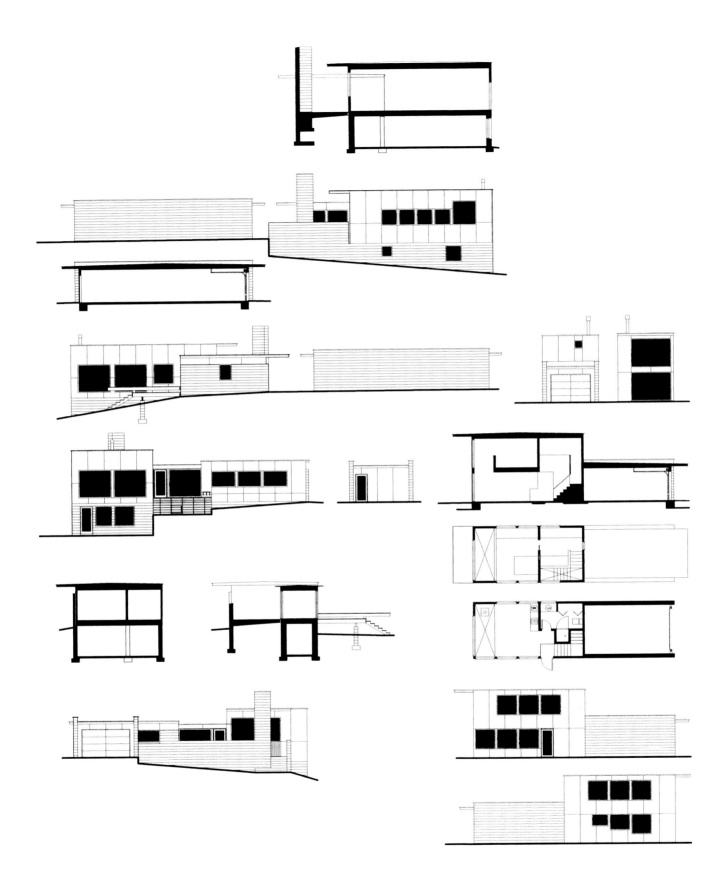

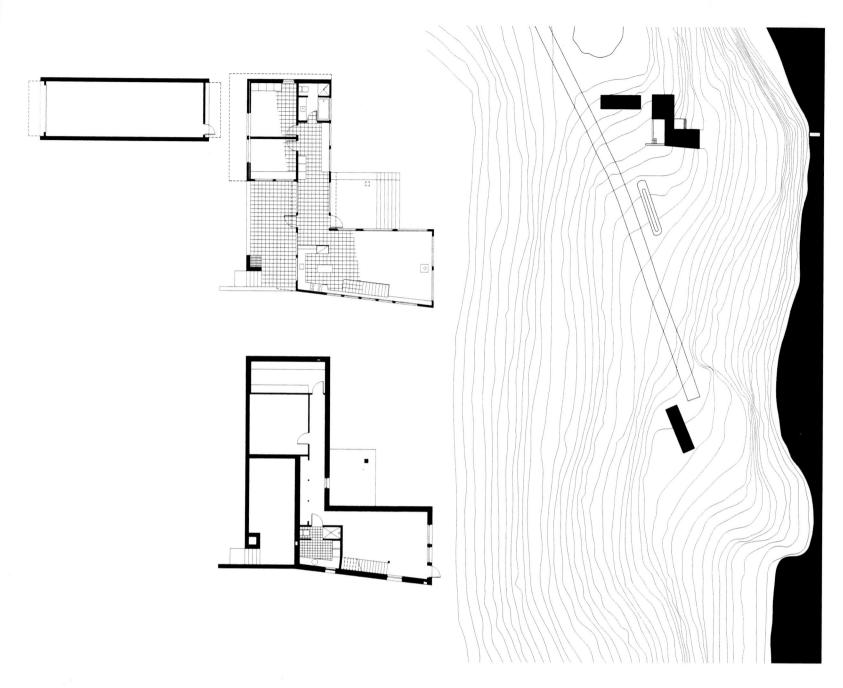

The Z-shaped plan of the main house separates
the living and sleeping areas, in contrast to the simple
rectangles of the garage and guesthouse.

above: The black Skatelite cladding and white masonry wall and chimney of this cabin complement the deep green of the forest and blue of the northern sky.

right: To the rear, the cabin opens out to the lake view with large wood-framed windows and an expansive wood deck and stairs that cascade down to the water.

HYYTINEN CABIN

COOK, MINNESOTA

FINNISH FIT

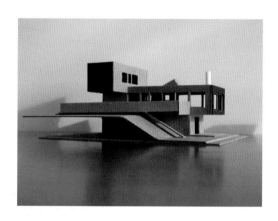

top: The cabin consists of two boxes perpendicular to each other, with one cantilevered over the slope and the other cantilevered over the entry deck.

above: The two boxes have narrow, horizontal lap siding along their sides, with black Skatelite cladding on the end walls and the splash line along the base.

The cabin David Salmela has designed for the Hyytinens on the site of a cabin they owned on Lake Vermillion is an essay in architectural drama. It shows Salmela's remarkable ability to take something as seemingly simple as a cabin by a lake and turn it into an almost uncanny catalog of modern forms and materials. The garage and boathouse, clad in black Skatelite, "will disappear in the woods," says Salmela, and draw you to the cabin, with its cantilevered second floor. Salmela has turned the box with the children's and guest bedrooms ninety degrees to the main cabin and projected it far over the entrance deck. "We tied the glulam beams back to the foundation, so the cantilever wasn't hard to do," says Salmela. "But it is dramatic." It also provides shade and shelter as you cross the deck to the front door, midway along the cabin, with a master bedroom to the left, bathrooms and kitchen straight ahead, and a living/dining space cantilevered over a concrete-block walkout basement. A range of cladding materials—black Skatelite along the splash line and on the end walls, narrow-lap horizontal cedar siding on the side walls, and vertical cedar slats along the railing—gives the cabin a modern, Scandinavian feeling, a quality fitting for this family of Finnish descent.

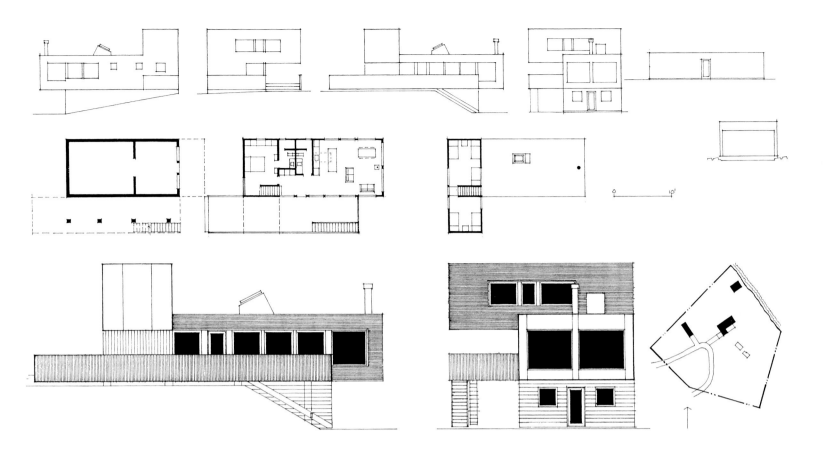

above: The plan has the main living spaces and master bedroom on one floor, with guest and children's bedrooms in the box above.

right: A wide set of stairs leads up from a black-clad garage and boathouse to a wood deck that projects out to the lake, enclosing a stair down to the water.

SINGLETON HILL HOUSE

MINNEAPOLIS, MINNESOTA

ON DIFFICULT GROUND

above: The house stands on a steep slope in an urban neighborhood, overlooking downtown Minneapolis through banks of large windows.

As we increase the density of cities, we will have to build on more difficult sites, land previous generations considered unbuildable. This house, which David Salmela designed for a couple in Minneapolis's Prospect Park, shows the potential of even the toughest terrain. Occupying the site of a former carriage house legally separated from its original property, the new house stands at the top of a very steep slope, with views of downtown Minneapolis to the west. The property has enough flat land to provide a plateau for cars, where Salmela also placed a small storage building partly cantilevered out over the retaining walls that step down the slope. With its rows of large windows, flat roofs, and minimal detailing, his design for the house recalls the spare, stuccoed structures of the International Style. A staircase inside the glass entrance door takes visitors down a half flight to the main floor, where a light-filled living/dining/kitchen space has glass doors leading out to a tree-shaded terrace also accessible via stairs from the parking area. Up half a flight from the entrance stand two bedrooms and two bathrooms, with an office and a lattice-covered terrace on the top floor. "It's one of the best urban houses I've done," says Salmela. And, as good design should, it makes a difficult site look easy.

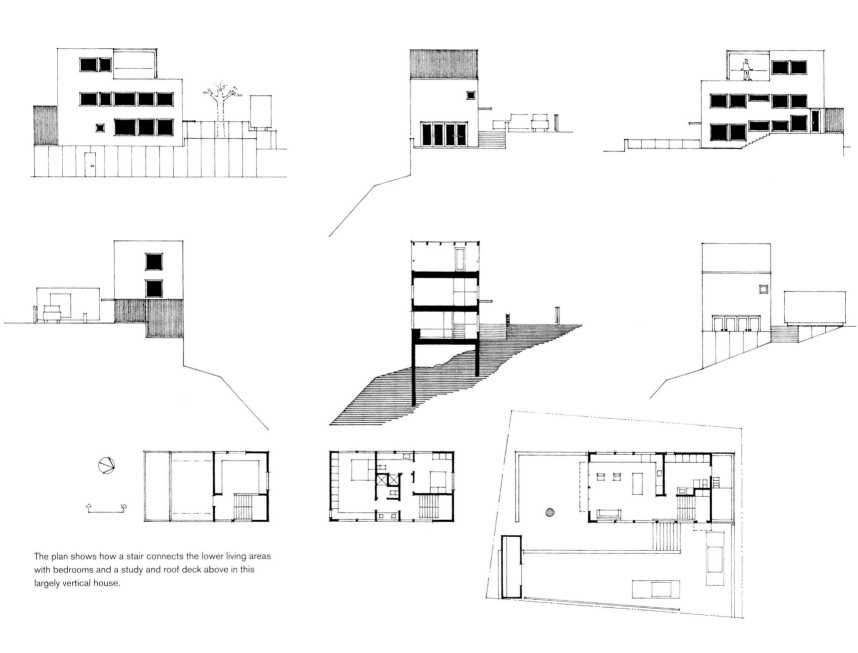

The plan shows how a stair connects the lower living areas with bedrooms and a study and roof deck above in this largely vertical house.

FRYKHOLM PHILLIPS HOUSE

GRAND RAPIDS, MICHIGAN

RAISING THE BAR

above: The bar containing the office and guest space extends along the entire length of the house, cantilevered at both ends and providing a view of the lake.

Steve Frykholm, the renowned graphic designer and creative director for Herman Miller, commissioned David Salmela to renovate a house that he and his interior-architect wife, Nancy Phillips, own on a large piece of land where they train and board horses. Salmela did several versions of the house; "it was hard to stop," he says. The third version, shown here in model form, has a two-car garage linked by a glassy entrance vestibule to the main living area of the house, containing a large bathroom/dressing area next to a master bedroom, with a dining area, living room, and kitchen all on one floor. Full-height windows offer a view of the adjacent pond, accessible from the house via a straight-run stair off the dining room. A long barlike structure extends over both the house and garage. With the office space for the owners as well as a guest bedroom and bathroom, the bar, square in section, has vertical standing-seam metal siding that contrasts with the black Skatelite cladding of the main house. "I designed it to be maintenance-free," says Salmela, "with a pure black box below and a shiny metal box on top." The syncopated rhythm of windows, the simplicity of forms, and the memorable quality of the second-floor cantilevered tube all seem fitting for an owner who has raised the bar, worldwide, for corporate graphic design.

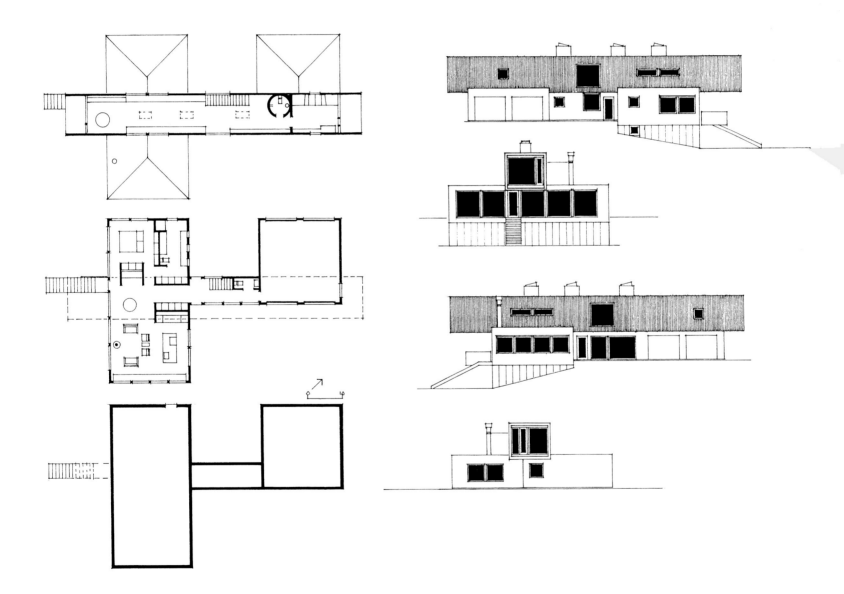

The second-story bar links the main floor (containing living
and sleeping spaces for the owners) to an attached garage
to the north.

SOLAR ARCHITECTURE

above: One of Salmela's largest, this house has four wings containing living spaces, a master bedroom, garages with bedrooms above, and a pool house.

All too often, solar panels look tacked onto buildings as an afterthought. David Salmela's design for the Zamzow house on a hilltop site overlooking Lake Superior to the south shows how solar panels can work well architecturally. Replacing a house that burned down, the Zamzow house has a cross-shaped plan. Visitors arrive at an auto court set into the hillside, with a pair of stairs leading up to a south-facing living/dining/kitchen wing that partly cantilevers over the parking area. A master bedroom suite occupies the east wing of the house and an indoor swimming pool, the west wing. The north wing contains a two-car garage and utility room, with two children's bedrooms and a recreation space above. A separate pottery building stands on the eastern terrace. Although large, the house has solar, daylighting, and materials strategies that reduce its environmental impact. Recycled zinc and environmentally friendly Skatelite panels clad the house, while large windows and rooftop lanterns bring ample amounts of light deep into the house. Meanwhile, black solar panels clad the south-facing wall of the second-story bedrooms as well as the south face of the raised rear walls of the swimming pool and the pottery shed. "Placing panels vertically," says Salmela, "is slightly less efficient, but they capture the low winter sun and are more easily integrated into the architecture."

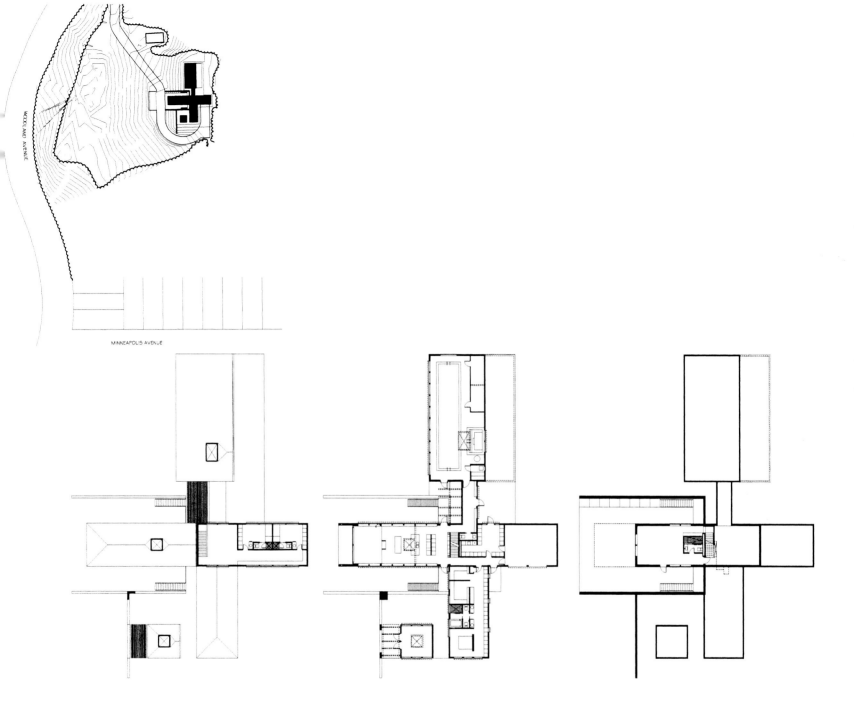

The cross-shaped plan shows the extent and complexity of
the house, with different functions in each wing clustered
around a central stair.

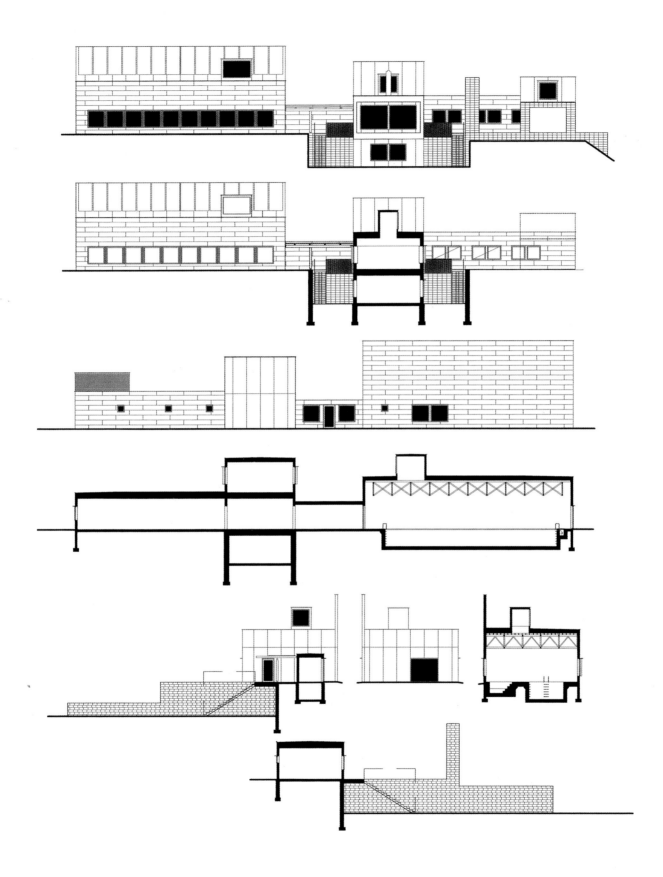

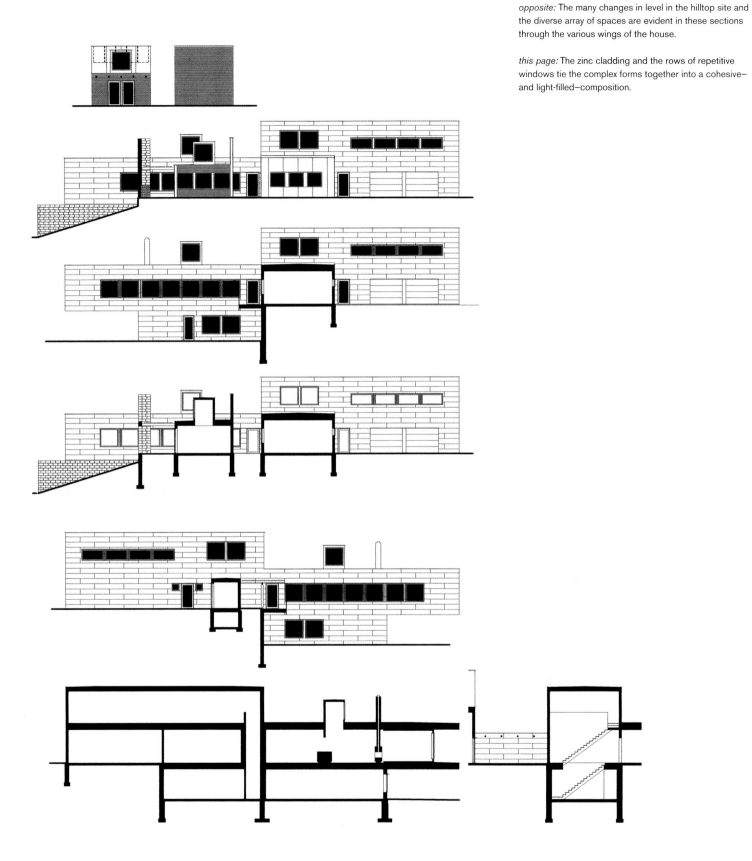

opposite: The many changes in level in the hilltop site and the diverse array of spaces are evident in these sections through the various wings of the house.

this page: The zinc cladding and the rows of repetitive windows tie the complex forms together into a cohesive—and light-filled—composition.

CAFESJIAN TOWER

ROSEVILLE, MINNESOTA

HIGH LIGHT

above: The tower attached to an existing house affords a variety of views and daylight conditions in a small and highly sculptural form.

Modern architecture excels at providing light-filled interiors by dispensing with wide, overhanging roofs and opening up rooms to the sun through large areas of glass. For Gerald Cafesjian, who wanted access to daylight not available in his existing house, David Salmela's architecture offered a way to achieve that, and so Cafesjian commissioned Salmela to design space in which he could enjoy the sun and view of Lake Josephine. Salmela raised the space above the trees in a tower, separated from the main house by a long deck and adjacent glass-enclosed sunroom. "The client is a major art collector," says Salmela, "and the sunroom would make a great sculpture gallery." The tower itself, clad in a smooth white stucco finish, has a two-story-high powder room at its base, along with an elevator and spiral stair that lead up to the doubly cantilevered sunroom. Variously sized windows provide different views of the surrounding landscape, while capturing the sun at different times of the day. Two rooftop boxes contain operable clerestory windows that naturally ventilate the entire tower by creating a chimney effect. Salmela calls the tower "Siza-like," referring to the simple, stuccoed buildings of Portuguese architect Alvaro Siza, but this tower is also a daring and expressive piece of habitable sculpture, making it, without a doubt, the largest work of art Cafesjian would own, were it built.

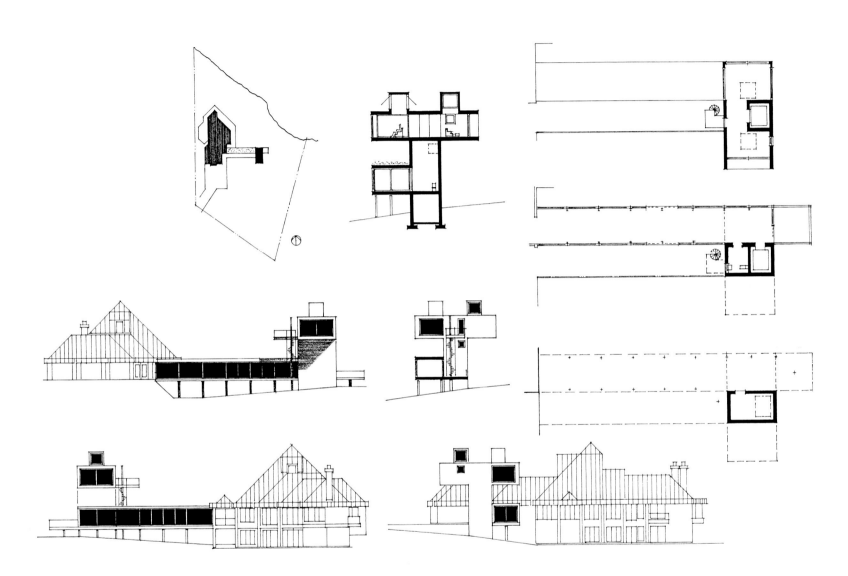

A glass-walled gallery connects the tower to the main house,
providing space for the owner's sculpture collection and
access to this new structure.

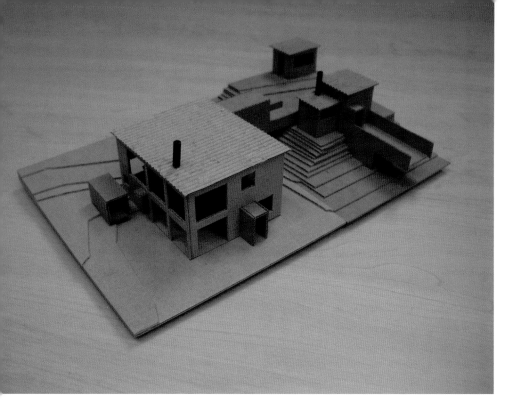

KOCH CABIN

A ROOM WITH A VIEW

above: This cabin stands on a high hill overlooking Lake Superior, with access over a bridge to the second-floor mezzanine, above the main living spaces.

Humans have long liked to climb hills and look out to distant views, but few of us get to live in such places, as Charles Koch will when he completes his cabin designed by David Salmela. Overlooking Palisade Head on Lake Superior, with commanding vistas to the north and north-east, "the cabin," says Salmela, "is all about the view." You enter the compound from above, past a storage building and sauna, with a cantilevered balcony extending out over the steep slope to the north. "The slats of the railing go to the ground," observes Salmela, "creating storage space underneath for essential things, like firewood and shovels." Farther down the hill, you come to a small, slat-enclosed bridge that leads to the cabin's second-floor entry. "It's very cabinlike inside," says Salmela, with a small bathroom, bedroom, and sitting area that can double as guest sleeping space, all separated by curtains and open to the living area below. A stair leads down to the combined kitchen, dining, and living room, whose full-height windows look out to the view and whose floor space is partly taken up by the exposed rock ledge on which the cabin stands. Contrasting with the structure's precision, that rock reinforces the sense Salmela wanted to create of a cabin "advanced and primitive at the same time."

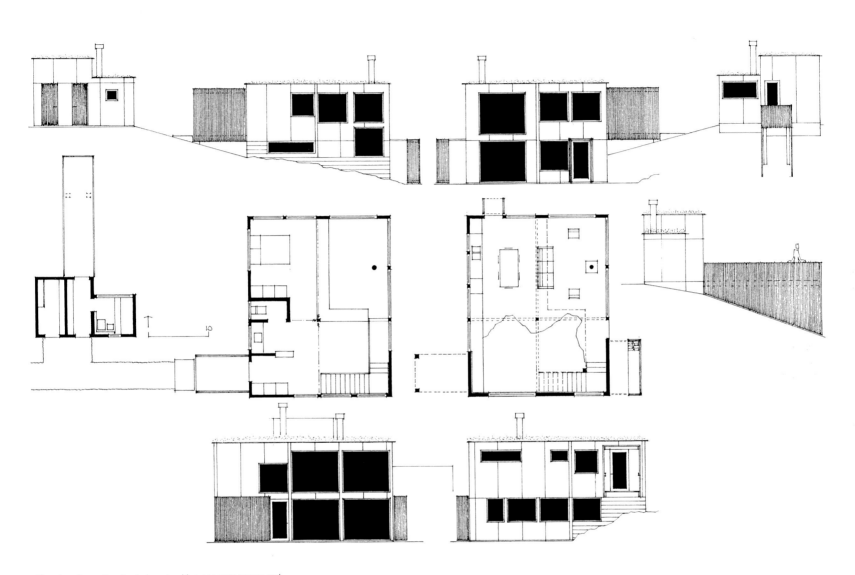

The plan shows the simple layout, with a separate sauna and
a bedroom and bath on the upper floor and a living/dining/
kitchen space below, with its own rock.

GABLES

FIVE POINTS OF A NEW ARCHITECTURE

In 1926, the architect Le Corbusier defined what he saw as the five most important features of modern architecture:

1. Buildings elevated on columns above the ground
2. Flat roofs able to support rooftop gardens
3. Flexible interior layouts with nonstructural partitions
4. Horizontal windows running the entire width of a space
5. Lightweight nonbearing exterior walls

Such features have become so common, especially in modern office and industrial buildings, that we can easily forget how radical these elements sounded at the time. Although they had already appeared on some buildings prior to 1926, Le Corbusier's "Five Points Toward a New Architecture" seemed so fundamental because of the metaphor behind it: the idea that a house—and by extension, any building—should be a "machine for living in."

We now know some of the consequences of living in and among machines. For most people, this has been a mixed blessing, with the two most common machines in our lives—automobiles and computers—having led to more isolation as well as more connection, more obesity as well as greater mobility. But the consequences for the natural world have been less equivocal. Whether we measure its effects in terms of environmental pollution, species extinction, or ecosystem destruction, the negative impacts of our highly mechanized modern life have started to threaten large parts of the planet and our own ability to thrive on it.

Viewed from the road, the cabin's striking zigzag roof looks as if it had been added to over time or dented by a falling tree.

The time has come for a new "five points," creating a more environmentally and socially responsible architecture than that envisioned by Le Corbusier. The modest cabin that David Salmela has designed for the Keel family in northern Minnesota provides one place to start. The Keel cabin seems to embrace some of Le Corbusier's five points, such as the concrete columns elevating the structure and the open plan with nonstructural partitions. But those features, and others, have a very different intent and meaning, making this cabin an ideal example of what a new five points of architecture might entail.

Rather than a machine, the Keel cabin seems more like a boat for living in. You come upon it suddenly, and the first thing you see is the cabin's metal roof shining in the sunlight. Like Le Corbusier's 1920s houses, with their brilliant white walls making them stand apart from the traditional buildings around them, this cabin clearly stands out from the thicket of trees and understory that surrounds it. And, echoing Le Corbusier's liking of naval design—the thin walls, flat roofs, metal stairs, and pipe railings of ships—the Keel cabin evokes a more modest maritime image. Its pitched roof recalls an overturned boat hull, with a kink along its length that has led neighbors to call it the "broken cabin," says Karl Keel.

As you approach the cabin down a short path, you begin to see the difference from what Le Corbusier advocated. Instead of the white exterior walls, flat roof, and uniform horizontal windows that Le Corbusier so liked, the Keel cabin has black cladding, a gabled roof, and differently sized square windows. But the contrast involves more than appearances. The more you learn about the Keel cabin and how it came about, the more you see in it a new five points of architecture, bringing modernism into a new and more responsible relation with the natural world.

1. Elevate Buildings to Leave the Land Undisturbed

While Le Corbusier's elevating buildings on columns did reduce the footprint of his structures, he also largely built in already disturbed, urban and suburban locations. For him, nature remained well tended for strolling parkgoers and sporting team players. The Keel cabin suggests something very different. Lifted above the slope that extends down to the nearby lake, the cabin lets the forest floor continue beneath it, with twelve concrete piers and a small mechanical enclosure barely interrupting the flow. High enough to enable wildlife to pass, and wide enough to provide

above: The interior of the cabin has a shiplike quality, with wood finishes, a galley kitchen, and a long, narrow proportion that make it feel like being on a boat.

top right: During the summer, the cabin's black cladding helps it disappear in the forest shade, while its metal roof and white-framed windows become more visible.

bottom right: On the lakeside, the cabin has a broad set of stairs that cascade out of the breezeway between the main house and guest quarters, like a frozen waterfall.

some shelter for animals in a storm, the cabin represents an architecture that hardly touches the land and barely affects the ecosystems that surround it. "We had to take down only two trees for the cabin," says Salmela.

2. Have Roofs Provide Habitat for Other Species

Le Corbusier's idea of rooftop gardens implied that those green spaces could compensate for the land taken up by a building, but here too, the implementation belied a different intention. Most of the rooftops he designed remained primarily hard surfaced, feeling more like urban plazas than gardens. The Keel cabin overcomes that urban bias, offering outdoor space for human and nonhuman alike. You enter the cabin through a broad covered breezeway, which divides the main living area from guest quarters. Wide stairs and long benches extend beyond the roof, enabling people to sit in the sun or shade, under cover or not, depending upon the weather. But above that space, the exposed wood trusses of the roof provide plenty of perch for passing birds that also might seek a place out of the rain. If, as Salmela observes, "The shiny roof appears to float above the cabin's black walls," so too does the roof give shelter to the winged creatures who actually do so.

3. Use as Little Interior Space as Possible

Le Corbusier admired ships not only for their aesthetic but also for their interior flexibility and compact use of space, even though many of the houses he designed for the relatively well-to-do had extensive floor plans that recalled traditional villas as much as they did passenger liners. The Keel cabin seems closer in spirit to the maritime metaphor. Salmela lined the interior—floor, walls, and ceiling—in birch, giving it the quality of a wood boat below deck, and he oriented the house toward views of the lake down the slope, accentuating the feeling from inside the cabin of floating up among the trees. The shiplike sensation gets enhanced by having all rooms occupy a single space, with living, dining, and kitchen areas on the main floor and a partitioned sleeping loft above, overlooking the entry and kitchen. The same shipshape quality occurs in the wood-lined guest quarters, where a single space, with a raised platform and exposed rafters, reinforces the feel of being in a boat. For family and friends who come to the cabin to fish, what could be better?

4. Reuse Windows to Reduce the Waste Stream

Le Corbusier depicted old objects in his paintings, but rarely did such things make it into his architecture, except as accessories in photos of his buildings. But reusing old things has since become almost a necessity, given how much energy, resources, and landfill we squander with our waste stream. The Keel cabin shows just how far reuse can go. Karl Keel spent several years going to reuse centers and window auctions. "I scrounged for almost everything," he says. That led Salmela to design around what the owners had already bought, ranging from the reused slate blackboards that become the kitchen counter to the extraordinary variety of windows Keel bought at auction, enabling the architects to include even a window for the cat at the floor. "The windows are exuberant and expressive," says Salmela, "but frugal at the same time."

An open porch, with a translucent roof to let in light, extends off the end of the cabin—so high in the trees that you have a sense of floating on a sea of green.

5. Have Exteriors That Accept Imperfections

Le Corbusier hoped, through his five points, to eliminate the unnecessary cost of traditional houses so that more people could afford a place to live. That admirable goal, however, often ran up against the added cost of making his early houses look machinelike, with hard-to-build smooth walls, flush windows, and no overhangs. The Keel cabin represents a different kind of affordability. Easily built, with ample overhangs and reveals, the exterior walls of the cabin consist of a low-cost black-painted plywood that has a smooth surface of wood dust mixed with a bonding glue. At the same time, the cabin looks anything but machinelike. As if for lack of enough paint, Salmela suggested that a few panels in the back of the house remain uncoated. "At first, it looked a little bizarre," chuckles Salmela, "but cabins should always look a little unfinished."

These five points of a new architecture may seem like a lot to load on such a simple cabin, but we have no choice. Given the damage our modern mechanized world has already done to the natural environment, we must move in a new, more affordable, more sustainable direction. Le Corbusier wrote at the end of his five-point manifesto that "nothing is left to us of the architecture of past epochs," and, as David Salmela has shown at the Keel cabin, that remains as true for us today as it was in 1926.

opposite top: Exposed roof trusses run the length of the upstairs bedrooms as well as along the length of the adjoining guest suite, expanding their sense of space.

opposite bottom: The large windows open up the interior to the outside, as does the glass entry door, which gives access to an outdoor breezeway designed for gathering.

this page: The elevations show the myriad windows, which were purchased by the owner ahead of time and accom-modated in the cabin's idiosyncratic design.

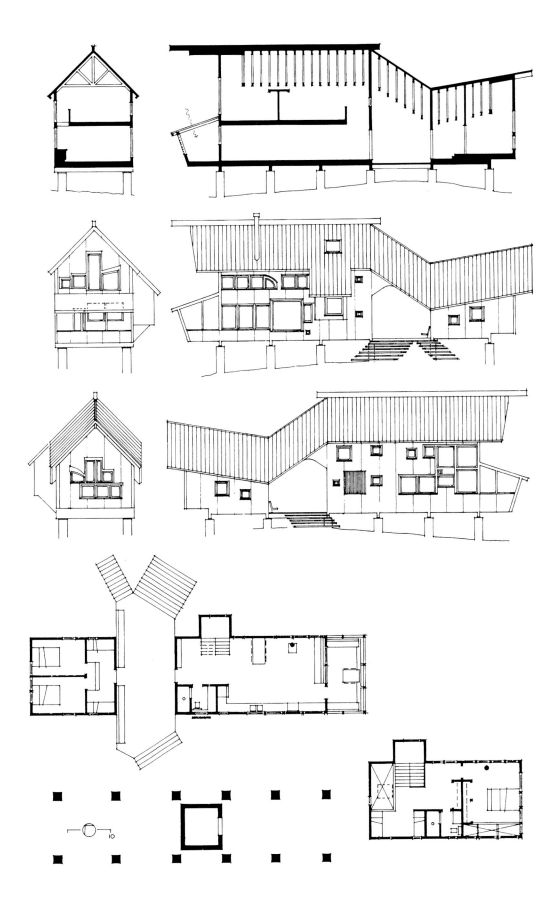

WONDERLAND

One of the continuing appeals of Lewis Carroll's *Alice's Adventures in Wonderland* comes from its having captured the feeling of being a child. Who hasn't, at some point in his or her youth, fantasized about a talking animal like the Cheshire Cat or feared an imperious adult such as the Queen of Hearts? One of the most common experiences conveyed in the book, however, involves the sense growing children have of feeling too big or too small in relation to the world around them, as Alice does when she shrinks after drinking from the bottle with the label that says "Drink me" or shoots up after eating from the cake marked "Eat Me." You realize, in reading the book, that for all our cultural or individual differences, we all once occupied the same state of childhood.

David Salmela's design of a house for the Andersons in Bayfield, Wisconsin, plays upon that shared experience. Standing in a historic district of old homes near the center of that picturesque port on Lake Superior, the house had to respect the white clapboarded, gable-roofed structures around it. But Salmela used that requirement to his advantage. Rather than quote too literally from the details of the houses next door, he refers instead to the drawings that children often make of a house, with large windows divided into four squares and a simple gable roof. Instead of referencing some specific period of time, the house evokes the condition, at once temporary and eternal, of being a child.

Other architects have made similar connections to the houses drawn by children, most notably Robert Venturi. But Salmela takes the idea much further than Venturi has done, down to the smallest details and even the furniture in the house. As in *Alice in Wonderland,* where every-

thing conspires to create a complete immersion in a fantastic world, so too in the Anderson house do elements hardly noticed in most residences seem unexpected and even somewhat startling when first encountered. And as happens with Alice, who gets accustomed to the unusual aspects of Wonderland, so too does the visitor to the Anderson house come to feel very much at home, much like a child again.

"I wanted it be a simple house with huge gestures," says Salmela, and he certainly achieved that. A two-car, gray-colored garage, with a guest suite above, faces the street and largely blocks the house and its side yard from view. And it signals Salmela's goal of "exaggerating everything." The garage's gable roof seems almost too large for that size structure, coming down low on either side, while the white-painted frieze board that runs under the eaves seems extrawide, colliding with the windows over the garage doors. The guest suite windows also carry on that hyperbole. On the street side, four four-square windows in a row seem to barely fit within the gable-end of the garage, while on the back side, four tiny square windows echo those in the front, while flanking the exterior door to the guest suite, with its grand stair leading up from the yard.

The garage gives the visitor a taste of what is to come in the main house. Down a narrow concrete path, you come upon a twenty-foot-wide stair with a deck and pergola at the top. More like a set of bleachers, the steps and the shade structure above seem intended for an audience to watch the events in the garden, like the caucus race in *Alice in Wonderland,* where the animals run whenever they feel like it and everyone wins. Salmela has designed a sauna building that will face the stairs across the yard and that, when built, will define an outdoor space ideal for gatherings in this small town, a kind of agora for agrarians.

top: In keeping with the scale-jumps in this house, the entry stairs are extra wide, turning them into an amphitheater ideal for family gatherings.

bottom: The side of the house facing the woods has an outdoor deck and screened porch, with large operable windows in the main living areas.

top: The eat-in kitchen has a wall of cabinets and a central table for informal dining with views of the woods that envelope the rear of the house.

bottom: Although traditional in form, the house has a clean, modern interior with large amounts of glass and classic Scandinavian furniture.

opposite: The plan of the house remains as simple as its form, with a central stair dividing the main house into two rooms on each floor.

Inside the door at the top of the stairs, you enter a narrow hall with a stair immediately in front of you, a living room to your left, and a kitchen/dining room to your right. "I wanted it to feel like an old house that had been updated," says Salmela, "with an old-fashioned eat-in kitchen and coats hung on pegs." The bare wood floors, white-painted woodwork, and simple central stair all reinforce that sense of the new-as-old. But it isn't long before the *Alice in Wonderland* quality of the place returns. In the living room, as well as in the family room above it, the windows have the proportion of historic windows, with four panes each, but the openings extend from floor to ceiling, providing a view of the water to the southeast, while also reminding the visitor of what it felt like to be young in a world of outsized things. The same happens with the furniture in the living room. The Andersons have placed generously sized chairs around a large table that is the same as the dining table (except that its legs are partly sawn off), bringing to mind that point in our childhoods when coffee tables seemed king-size.

The screened porch and deck on the opposite side of the eighteen-foot-wide house also play upon our sense of size and scale. The railing around the porch, for example, has extrawide boards, which offer greater privacy as well as a sense of how things look from the perspective of a child in terms of safety and security. That side of the house also looks out to a thickly wooded hillside whose sheer greenness comes through most vividly on the upper floor of the house, where a large square window in the master bedroom looks like a framed nature photograph. But after all the humor in the house, you begin to wonder, looking out at the woods, if you would be at all surprised to see a Cheshire Cat up in a tree, smiling back at you.

"I wanted to bring the modern and the traditional together," says Salmela, recognizing that the house could be seen as "nostalgic, which is not a good word among architects." And yet, he adds, "we have to respect nostalgia, because we are always recollecting something from the past in order to create something new." But the Anderson house suggests something more profound than simple nostalgia, with its self-conscious attention to the past. As Lewis Carroll did in *Alice in Wonderland,* David Salmela has touched in this house some of the deepest chords of our common childhood, part of the collective subconscious that we all carry with us into adulthood and that we remember, not deliberately, but despite ourselves, when triggered by things that evoke the feeling of being small. "The town loves the house," says Salmela, "because it fits the historic district while remaining modern." It also fits with the wonder that we have all experienced at some point in our youth, and what is there not to love about that?

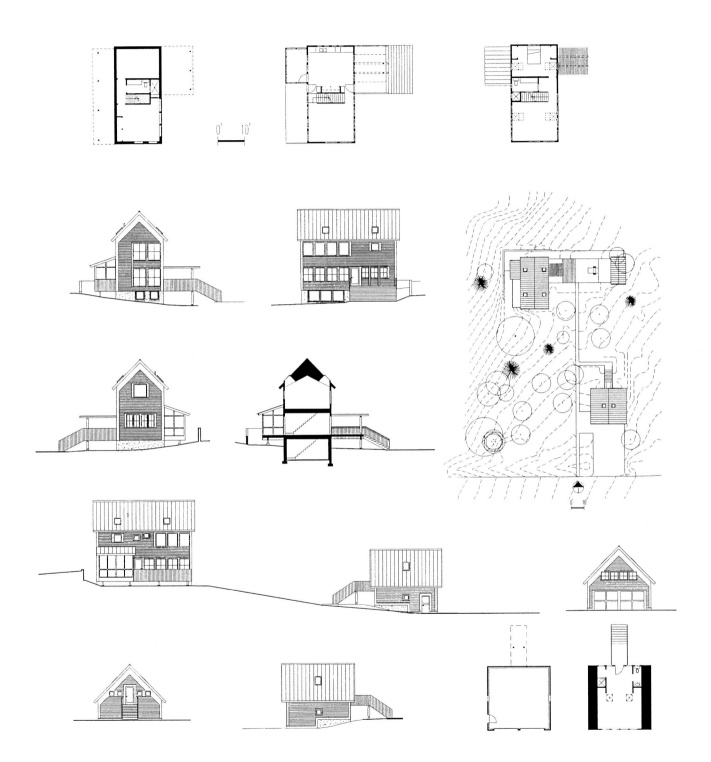

TRACINGS

Architects used to spend a lot of time tracing, putting one layer of translucent tracing paper over another, redrawing some lines and rethinking others as a design developed. Computers have largely replaced that activity, as digital lines on a screen come and go without a trace, and that ability has certainly made architects more efficient. But something has disappeared along with the tracing paper in architects' offices: the sense of design being an act of carefully layering the new onto the old, of respecting what exists while reinterpreting it in terms of what could be. In the push for ever-greater efficiency, we have also created a more ephemeral way of working that may not sufficiently value the past and the new vision that can arise from the traces it leaves behind.

That idea may seem like a vestige from the past, at least to a new generation of professionals. In most architectural offices, the younger staff members all use computers to do most of their designing and drawing, even as older members of firms still sometimes use tracing paper to draw. A person skilled at the latter, like David Salmela, can often match the speed of the former, but as with office workers everywhere, most architects recognize that the computer has already become the dominant means of production and that tracing paper will someday go the way of the T-square, triangle, and other formerly essential tools of the trade. With that change in technology, though, we need to rediscover the meaning of tracing, for, as Marshall McLuhan once said, every new technology turns the old one into an art form.

The art of tracing comes through in Salmela's additions to and modifications of the Deloia house. The original house consisted of a conventional Cape Cod design: a modest gable-roofed house with dormers for the second-floor bedrooms and an attached two-car garage on one side. Set back from the road on a large, wooded piece of land that slopes down to a river, the house needed updating after years of service as the Deloias raised their family. "We wanted to open up the Cape in all four directions," says Salmela, "to connect the original house to the outdoors." In doing so, he also reinterpreted the house in imaginative ways, letting the traces of the older structure suggest the character and qualities of the new insertions.

This act of tracing echoes the work of his client, David Salmela's dentist, Gary Deloia. Like architects, dentists work from both physical and photographic impressions of existing conditions when inserting something new, such as a cap or filling. And like architects, dentists also have to work with exacting care to ensure that the new seems to fit seamlessly with the old. The art of dentistry lies not in drawing attention to itself or creating a radical departure from what has gone before, but in just the opposite: doing what needs to be done in the hope that it disappears without a trace.

opposite top: The approach to the house includes two
outbuildings (a garage and a workshop) by the side of the
road, common in that rural area.

opposite bottom: The outbuildings by the road provide
a sense of privacy and enclosure for the house that makes
the front yard a more useable outdoor space.

above: The paved auto court has a brick walk that beckons
visitors along the stone wall and up a couple of steps to
the front entry terrace.

top: The new Salmela-designed entry trellis and flanking benches enlarge the scale of the existing front door on the original Cape Cod–style house.

bottom: On one side, Salmela designed a study attached to the master bedroom and, at the rear, he added a white wood-framed screened porch.

The new study has expanses of glass on all sides, including skylights and a glazed link back to the existing house and master bedroom suite.

Salmela and his colleagues, including the landscape architect Shane Coen and contractor Bob Bell, have matched that same level of skill in the Deloia house. The test: you can drive right by the house without noticing anything new, even though a lot has changed. Salmela placed two new, gable-roofed, clapboarded buildings close to the road, one serving as a garage and the other as a workshop. Their location might appear to draw your eye, but because many of the farms in the area have similar structures near the road to shorten the length of driveways, the new buildings end up fooling the eye by blending right in. Tracing what we expect to see can be as effective as tracing something once there. The two buildings, standing on either side of the driveway like two sentinels, also partly block the view of the front yard, with its new stone walls and plantings leading visitors to the entry. "I wasn't sure I liked the two buildings there at first," says Linda Deloia, "but they have made our front yard so much more useful because of the privacy they have given us. We use it like we never did before."

The same could be said of the house itself. The trace of the original structure's simple gabled form is echoed in the new gabled pergola over the front door as well as in the gabled office addition to the west and the gabled screened porch added to the rear of the house. Those enlargements have enabled the Deloias to enjoy their land in ways not possible before, whether eating on the two-story-high porch or watching the seasons change through the five-foot-square office windows. The insertion of new windows into existing openings, the replacement of former picture windows on the front of the house, and the installation of large, floor-to-ceiling glass on the back all serve to reorient the house toward the wood deck and wooded back yard. "We've rediscovered what we have here," says Linda Deloia.

A further opening up has happened on the interior. Salmela created a master bedroom suite with an expanded bathroom and widened hallway connecting the office addition to the front foyer, whose new white-painted stair and railing brighten the entire entrance. The opening up of walls between the living, dining, and kitchen areas also extends the view through the house to the outdoors and makes the whole house feel much larger. A series of deep-set windows around two sides of the new kitchen allow an expanded view out to the front of the house, while providing a place for people to sit and talk during the preparation of meals. Nothing feels forced or out of character, and yet almost everything on the main level has been rethought or realigned to create something new.

The artfulness with which the designers have blended new elements into the existing house and landscape offers a model of what many architects may face in the future. In a period in which loans for buildings may become more difficult to secure, and in which the resources for building may become scarcer and more expensive, reusing what we already have will likely become much more common. That may, in turn, lead architects to rethink what it means to trace. While technology may make tracing less common in the office, the technique may be applied more to projects as the profession works more often with what exists, layering the new over the old. And with it, architects might also learn something from dentists, whose work leaves no noticeable sign. That ideal may be impossible to achieve in full, given the size and visibility of what architects do, but it serves as a worthy goal and one that architects, for thousands of years, managed to achieve, given all the buildings from the past for which we have no physical remains. Such humility may, in the end, be the real lesson of the Deloia house: to do so much work while leaving so little trace.

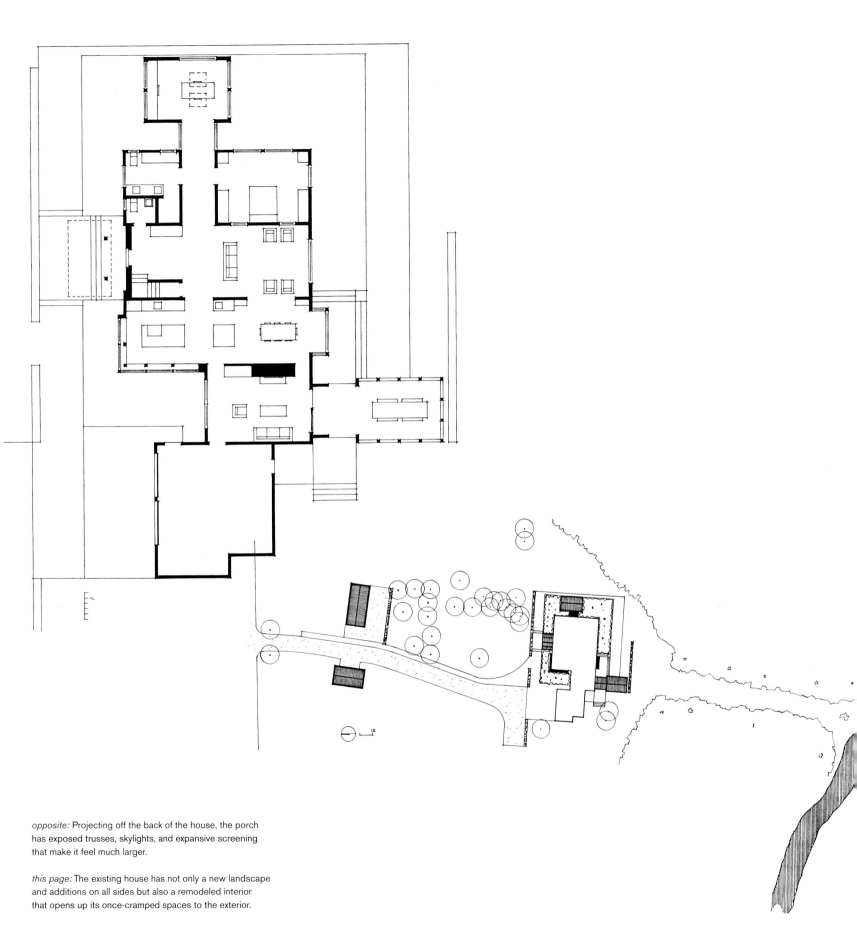

opposite: Projecting off the back of the house, the porch has exposed trusses, skylights, and expansive screening that make it feel much larger.

this page: The existing house has not only a new landscape and additions on all sides but also a remodeled interior that opens up its once-cramped spaces to the exterior.

HEALTH AND HOME

Architects have a habit of imagining the plans of buildings by examining their exteriors. That happens out of necessity in many cases, since most buildings are privately owned and remain inaccessible to most passersby. But that "X-ray" vision, as some architects call it, of seeing through the outer skin of a building to visualize the spaces and structure within, has the added benefit of training the eye to detect an internal problem through some minor external detail, as well as training the mind to think three-dimensionally based on the indications of a two-dimensional exterior surface. In this capacity, architects share a lot with doctors. Physicians also become adept at gauging possible problems with the internal systems and structures of our bodies from assessing the signs or symptoms we exhibit externally. And they, too, have X-ray vision, aided by imaging technologies of various kinds, for looking inside the body for possible disease or dysfunction.

The house that David Salmela designed for the physicians David and Judy Arvold brings that shared way of seeing to mind. The house sits as a compact form on its hillside site, overlooking Lake Superior and downtown Duluth in the distance. With a cedar-shake gable roof parallel to the road, the house looks, at first glance, like a conventional, white-painted colonial of the sort you often see in new residential developments, complete with the two-car garage joined to the main house by a pergola-covered breezeway. But on closer examination, the house conveys on its exterior an internal organization far different from what you might expect.

Unlike the typical suburban house, with a front lawn, foundation shrubs, and walkway that few people use, the Arvold house defies expectations with a series of layers between the house and

road—a row of tall grasses, a line of trees, and a low wall enclosing a grass terrace fit for outdoor dining or lounging. Those layers, like veils in front of the main body of the house, suggest a more functional approach to the way we represent ourselves to the world. Rather than the standard-issue uniform of grass and shrubs, meant to express solidarity with the identical attire in front of neighbors' houses, the Arvolds' yard serves several real needs— providing a visual screen for the house, an outdoor gathering place for the family, and even a tall-grass habitat for small animals displaced from the neighbors' turf lawns. Like doctors' scrubs, the Arvolds' yard attire might seem scruffy to some, but it does its job well, with minimal maintenance.

The house itself also defies expectations, for very good reasons. As you examine the house, you first notice the lack of a front door. Most people, of course, hardly ever use their front doors, entering their houses from their garages, and so Salmela has simply accepted that fact and placed the front and back doors facing the garage across the narrow breezeway and deck that extends out back. That pergola-covered space, along with a similar one on the other side of the house, offers ample opportunity for sitting outside, while expanding the living area of what remains, especially in its suburban location, a relatively compact structure. The Arvolds' residence reminds us that human health has as much to do with the quality of the environment around us as it does with what's inside.

What's inside the house reads on its exterior in ways that few structures allow. The facade, for example, has a row of small square windows equally spaced along the board-and-batten upper level, clearly conveying the small service spaces—closet, stair, and bathrooms—along that side of the second floor. Likewise, the main level has a series of high, foursquare windows along the front elevation, indicating the circulation route that runs along that side of the house, with three, large sheets of glass providing visual punctuation. That large glass area recalls the picture windows that occur so frequently in suburban houses, although these three openings offer a sight of only the main stair, with its white baluster screen blocking the view into the main living area. Who needs drapes when you have a beautifully designed staircase to look at?

above: From below, the projecting living room and entry deck seem to reach out to the view, aided by the large windows along the rear wall.

right: The main stair, with its white-slat screen, lets in light to the lower level while providing visual privacy to the entry hall, kitchen, and dining room.

That three-part picture window also reflects, on the outside of the house, the large kitchen and dining area behind the stair, with their tall windows along the back elevation offering a view of water and sky. Meanwhile, three smaller windows along the facade echo the more private family and living room spaces that extend through the house and out a projecting bay in the back. At the center of the house, between the dining and living areas, stands an enormous, sculptural, stuccoed fireplace with back-to-back openings. That double fireplace looks as well as functions like the veritable heart of the house, warming the other spaces and throbbing with the life that it gathers around it.

"The house is a play of symmetry and asymmetry," says David Salmela, and that idea applies to the internal functions of the house as much as to its exterior composition. The asymmetrical arrangement of windows and rooms on the main level reflects the dynamic qualities of the house during the day and evening, while the symmetrical, repetitive patterns of square windows on the second floor, both in the front and back, evoke the more static nature of a household at night. As with the body, so too in a building do the cycles of day and night—of activity and rest, production and consumption, community and privacy—represent a healthy life, something that both doctors and architects, each in their own way, can help us achieve.

One of the most telling features of the house is David Arvold's figural carvings in the wood pilasters on the first floor, depicting people intertwined with trees and vines. Recalling the relief sculptures in medieval Scandinavian stave churches, his work gives the house a hand-crafted quality rarely seen in modern structures. But it also reminds us of the deep connection between medicine and architecture. Bodies and buildings have always been extensions of and

To maximize the view, Salmela placed the main spaces along the back of the house, with windows that extend above the ceiling.

metaphors for each other, with each having skin, structure, systems, and spaces that all serve specialized roles in the maintenance of our daily lives. And as we see in the Arvolds' house—in both its design and in its carvings—the more care we take with our bodies and our buildings, the better off we will be.

above: The double-sided masonry fireplace, with its shaped stucco form, serves as the heart of the house, radiating warmth throughout the living spaces.

opposite: Despite its traditional gabled form, the plan of the house has open spaces that flow into each other with a simplicity that reflects Salmela's modern roots.

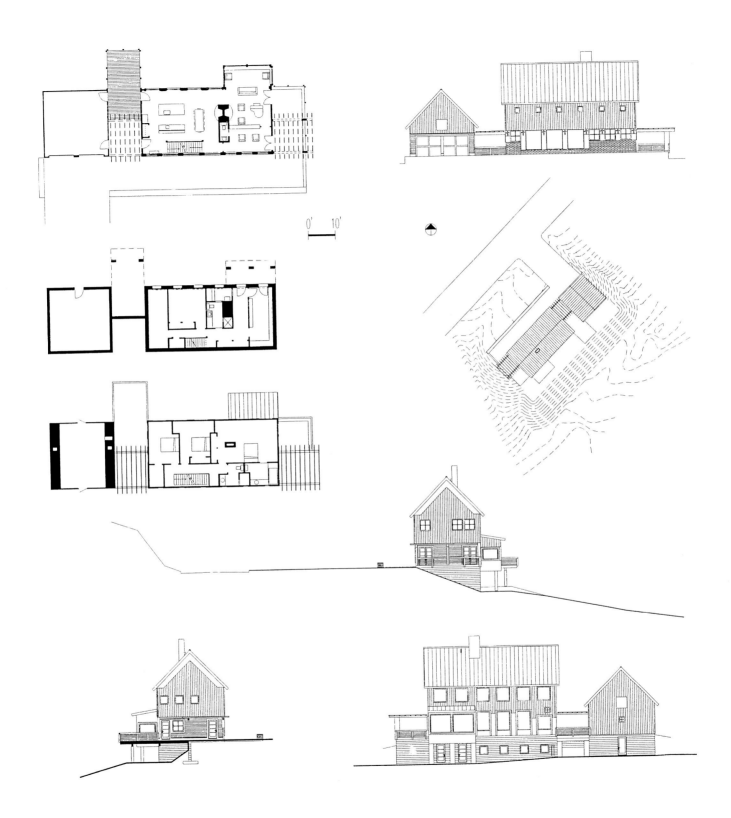

0'   10'

EXTENDED FAMILY

We have spent most of our history as a species living in close proximity within large families. Grandfathers and grandmothers, aunts and uncles, cousins and siblings, nephews and nieces— such extended groups of relatives offered adults a variety of confidants and cohorts and children a variety of caregivers and companions. The postindustrial economy has made it much harder to maintain such connections as we pursue job opportunities and career moves that often take us far from where we grew up. And with the loss of large extended families all in one place has come the loss of the compounds that once characterized human settlements, with clusters of houses all owned by members of the same clan.

That makes this cabin that David Salmela designed for Jim and Colleen Ryan's family as fascinating socially as it is architecturally. Jim Ryan, who led the family's construction and development company until his death in 2009, served as a kind of patriarch of his firm as well as his family. "Jim always went the extra mile to show employees he cared," remembered Ryan employee Mike Ernst. "He enjoyed meeting our children and knew our spouses by name." That same caring for other people pervades the cabin that Jim Ryan had Salmela design next to the houses of his relatives on Lake Esquagama in northern Minnesota.

"I think of the Ryans' place as a Minnesota version of something Robert Venturi might have done," says Salmela. Venturi, along with his partners Denise Scott Brown and Steve Izenhour, became famous in the 1960s for inventive interpretations of vernacular American architecture, using the forms and materials that had become common in ordinary buildings across the country, while exaggerating their features and expanding their scale in ways that recalled the pop art of that era.

below: On its lakeside promontory, the cabin stands behind two outbuildings (a storage shed and a two-story guest-house) that shield it from neighbors.

opposite, top: The approach to the cabin's front door from the parking area proceeds down a straight walk past newly planted trees and between the two outbuildings.

opposite, middle: The rear of the house features a white exterior chimney serving the back terrace and rows of windows that connect the interior to the lake.

opposite, bottom: The gabled roofs of the buildings give them a traditional quality, while the simple detailing and large windows convey their modernity.

Salmela has done much the same at the Ryan cabin, playing with familiar forms while diminishing their size and amplifying their scale. This pattern is clear the moment you leave your car in the driveway. Salmela and his landscape architect, Robert Close, situated the group of small structures so that you approach them down a straight and narrow concrete walk, with newly planted trees on either side that provide visual privacy along with a grand sense of arrival.

That mix of small size and large scale continues in the structures themselves. The walk takes you between two diminutive buildings: a one-story garage on the right for the Ryans' golf cart and a two-story bunkhouse for the children of the Ryans' extended family on the left. The latter seems perfectly scaled for its inhabitants. With a small bathroom and storage area on the first floor, the bunkhouse has a narrow stair that leads up to a wood-lined room, well lit by a continuous row of wood windows, with four beds cleverly arranged in the small space. It functions remarkably well and yet it has the feel of a childhood fantasy, like living in a full-sized playhouse.

The main house has some of the same quality. On the main level, it has essentially one large room, carefully divided into different areas through the manipulation of the floor plan. You enter the house on axis with the entry walk. On one side is a small toilet room and on the other is a mechanical room, with a straight-run stair leading up to the second floor right in front of you. To the right, an elegant kitchen opens out to a corner dining area, whose expansive windows and French doors lead to the bluestone terrace that Robert Close designed to encompass the house. Directly behind the stair stands a fireplace, with space for seating looking out to the lake. A living area occupies the other corner of the house, backed up by a space designed for watching television. "The house had to occupy the footprint of the previous cabin," observes Salmela, but he has made what was once a closed and somewhat claustrophobic structure into an open and light-filled space.

A straight-run stair leads to the bedrooms above and divides the main floor into a kitchen/dining area on one side and living spaces on the other.

That intention is evident on the second floor. Double skylights with a light reflector between them flood the stairwell and the center of the house with daylight. At the top of the stairs, you find two master bedroom suites on either side of the landing, each with its own bathroom and closets and each with projecting, walk-in window bays that expand the bedrooms while keeping the house within its required footprint. "It's a traditional house," says Salmela, referring to its central stair and symmetrical second-floor plan, "and a modern one too," with its large windows and extended living space for this large family.

The exterior of the house reflects that combination of tradition and modernity, once again playing with the size and scale of otherwise ordinary materials. Salmela has arranged common cladding materials in ways that "emphasize the planes of the house," as he puts it. The entry facade, with its one-story shed roof projection lowering the apparent height of the house, has board-and-batten cladding, in contrast to the tongue-and-groove siding on the upper floor. That pattern shift makes the lower level feel closer and the upper level farther away, enlarging the perceived size of this small house. A similar play of clapboard patterns occurs on the side of the house, where traditional lap siding contrasts with the modern flush-board enclosures of the projecting bays on the second floor.

As humans, we extend our lives through our families, knowing that our children and grandchildren will carry on what we have handed down to them. But we can also do that through architecture. While Jim Ryan barely had time to enjoy the cabin he commissioned David Salmela and Robert Close to design for his extended family, he left behind something his children and grandchildren will long enjoy and his relatives will long remember him by.

At the same time Salmela and Close have created a compound that recalls the structures that once defined multigeneration families, with multiple buildings arranged in ways that allow for proximity and privacy at the same time. While the smaller nuclear families that characterize most modern households have little need for bunkhouses or more than one master bedroom, the Ryans' cabin complex shows how humans have long lived and how many of us may someday live again. In a world in which economic uncertainty may lead families to live in more mutually supportive and self-sustaining ways, and technological mobility may allow employees to work in a more physically distant and digitally enhanced manner, one of the most traditional forms of human relationships—the extended family—could become one of the most modern ways of living as well, an idea in this cabin complex that Jim Ryan has left behind for us all.

above: Although all one room, the main space has a series of seating areas to accommodate different activities, like enjoying a fire, the television, or the lake.

right: The upstairs bedrooms have full-height windows in projecting bays that seem to extend the spaces into the lake and surrounding trees.

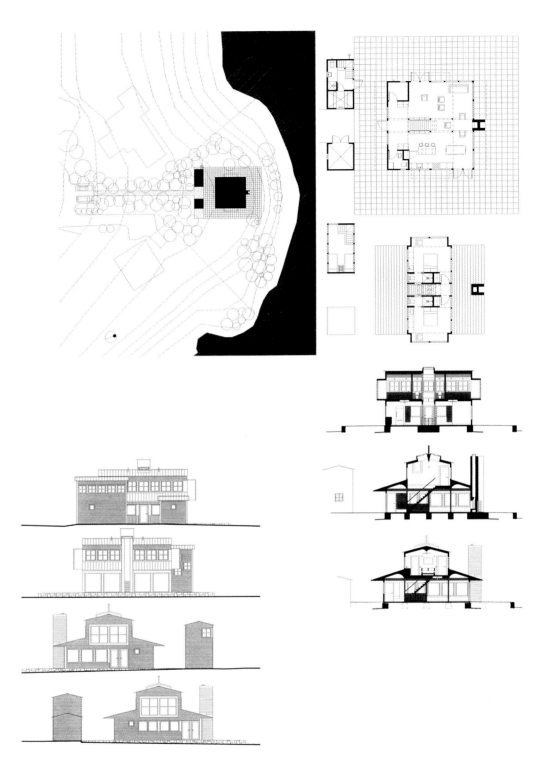

left: The two bedroom suites have low counters for storage and matching bathrooms with small interior windows that grab light from the stair.

above: The cabin has a simple square shape on a rectangular terrace, with a play of symmetry and asymmetry in its elevations and site plan.

JOHNSON HEDLUND HOUSE

DULUTH, MINNESOTA

DOUBLE CANTILEVER

above: The metal roof and zinc-clad exterior, as well as the large asymmetrical windows, contrast with the traditional gabled forms of the house.

Designed for a structural engineer, his physician wife, and their three children, this house has a double cantilever, in which the upper bedroom floor projects out over the lower living/dining/ kitchen room along both its length and width. "The bedrooms simply needed more space than the living area," says Salmela. That double cantilever certainly creates drama as you drive up to the house, with its black-slate-clad lower floor appearing darker and heavier than the shimmering zinc-clad upper floor it supports. You enter the house through a glass-walled link that connects the primary structure with a long perpendicular wing with a three-car garage, guest and utility rooms, and an upstairs office. The living spaces run the length of the main house, with a stair up to the four bedrooms above and another stair down to a large basement with a recreational space that looks out to large light wells at either end of the house. Throughout, features like a balcony supported on a single column and large windows and skylights provide unexpected views of the surrounding landscape. The house's structural daring seems entirely appropriate for the residence of a structural engineer, just as its double cantilever seems like a fitting symbol for the way we all have to stretch these days to balance the many demands of modern life.

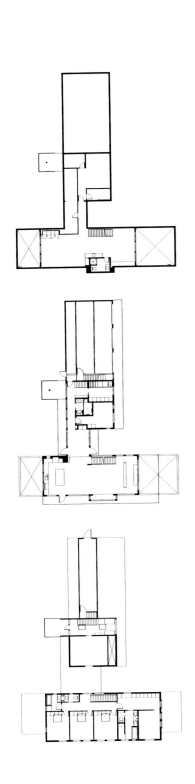

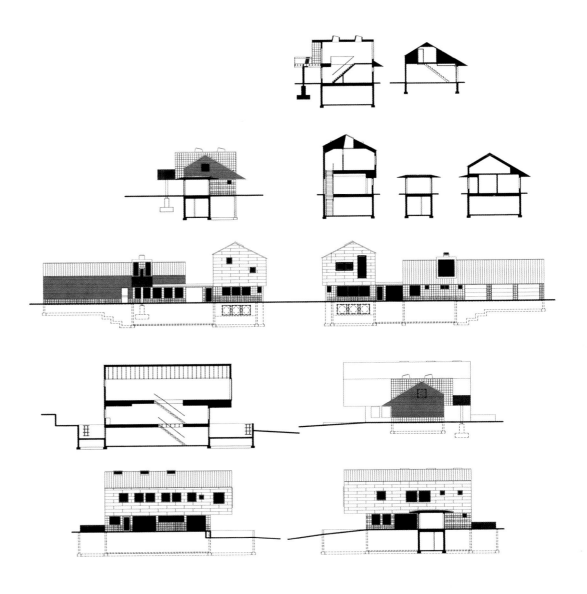

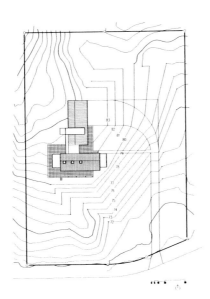

top: The house has a highly energetic massing, with a cantilevered upper floor, a boxlike dormer office above the garage, and asymmetrical windows.

bottom: Its T-shaped plan divides the main living and sleeping spaces in the house from the more public garage, guest, and office wing to the rear.

ANDERSON LANDSCAPE AND SAUNA

DULUTH, MINNESOTA

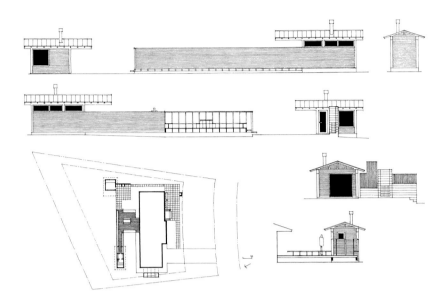

OUTDOORS

top: Additions on all sides of the house (including a front fireplace and terrace, a wood shed, a meditation room, and a sauna) fully utilize the site.

above: Standing at the back of the existing house, the deck, screen-wall bench, and gabled sauna create an outdoor room that expands the living space.

The landscape around most suburban houses goes to waste, with expansive lawns that get little use and demand a lot of care. The Andersons, whose house in Bayfield, Wisconsin, David Salmela also designed, hired him to rethink the landscape around their ranch-style house in Duluth. Conceiving of the project as a series of outdoor rooms, Salmela added a pervious-paved terrace and masonry fire pit to the front of the house, providing the owners with a place to sit in the evening, to look out to Lake Superior to the south, and to greet their neighbors as they walk by. It makes the front yard functional. A wood-framed, wood-storage shed occupies one side yard. Along the other side yard, pervious pavers provide a link between the front yard and back, which has another fire pit and an adjoining meditation room, whose large windows and broad, shallow-gable roof give the twelve-foot-square structure real presence. Salmela replaced the existing backyard deck with a larger wood deck, whose extensive built-in benches and wood-slat privacy screen lead to a small sauna building, with high windows and broad gable roof. Salmela also had the rear of the house painted a deep blue, a backdrop that gives the entire ensemble the feel of a stage ready made for an outdoor performance.

HOLMES PROTOTYPE CABIN

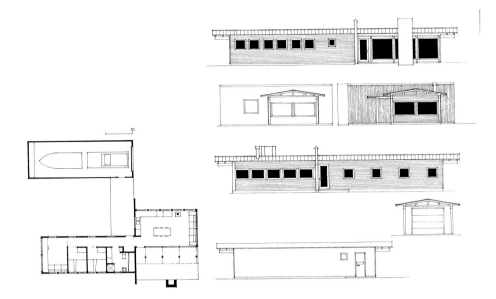

CONTRACTOR-FRIENDLY CABIN

top: The plan consists of two parts: a long bedroom wing with generous windows that expand the small rooms, and a large living/dining/kitchen space.

above: Designed for ease of construction at a minimal cost, this prototype cabin has a shallow gable roof, a low eave, and a simple structure with ample glazing.

Architects do not always design buildings with contractors in mind, which can lead to tensions between the two professions. David Salmela and his longtime contractor, Brad Holmes, have a very different relationship, evident in this prototype cabin that Salmela designed for Rod & Sons Carpentry to build on lots Holmes owned. "It's one story, low enough to build from the ground," says Salmela, "with a sloped metal roof shallow enough that you can stand on it without needing scaffolding." That concern for ease of construction carries through the entire cabin. It has a single, window-lined kitchen/dining/living room offset from a wing that contains three bedrooms, a bathroom, and a mechanical closet. Offset gable roofs can be difficult to build, so Salmela separated the two with a wall that extends beyond them, making them easier to construct. "The wall has a small roof along its top, with an opening for birds," says Salmela, "like a big birdhouse." Meanwhile the garage, with space for a car and boat, stands apart from the main cabin, also simplifying its construction. This ability to design with contractors in mind comes from Salmela's extensive experience as an architect and from his long relationship with Brad Holmes, who builds many of his projects in northern Minnesota. This cabin is a prototype for architects and contractors everywhere.

FIORE CABIN

ELLISON BAY, WISCONSIN

LIFE'S ASYMMETRIES

above: The traditional shape of this cabin, with its telescoping gabled and shed roofs, contrasts with the modern, asymmetrical arrangement of its large windows.

We seek symmetries in life, even though we know, from our own faces in the mirror, that nothing is ever completely symmetrical. The cabin that David Salmela has designed for the Fiores, a physician couple, echoes that idea architecturally. The approach to the house is decidedly asymmetrical, with a drive that hugs the property boundary along a line of trees before turning toward the cabin in the middle of a beautiful field. As you drive toward the gable-roofed house, its facade has two large windows topped by two small ones that, like a face, are not quite aligned. From the parking area, you see how the cabin's roof steps down, from a high gable to a lower one and then to a shed roof at the rear, "like many of the barns in the area," says Salmela. While the collection of large and small windows on the side elevation lacks any symmetry as you approach the glass entrance door, the opposite wall has the same organization of openings, like the mirror image of eyes and ears on either side of a person's face. Inside, the slightly off-center location of the kitchen, bathroom, and fireplace in the high-ceilinged living space reflects those exterior asymmetries, all of which make this cabin so appealingly human.

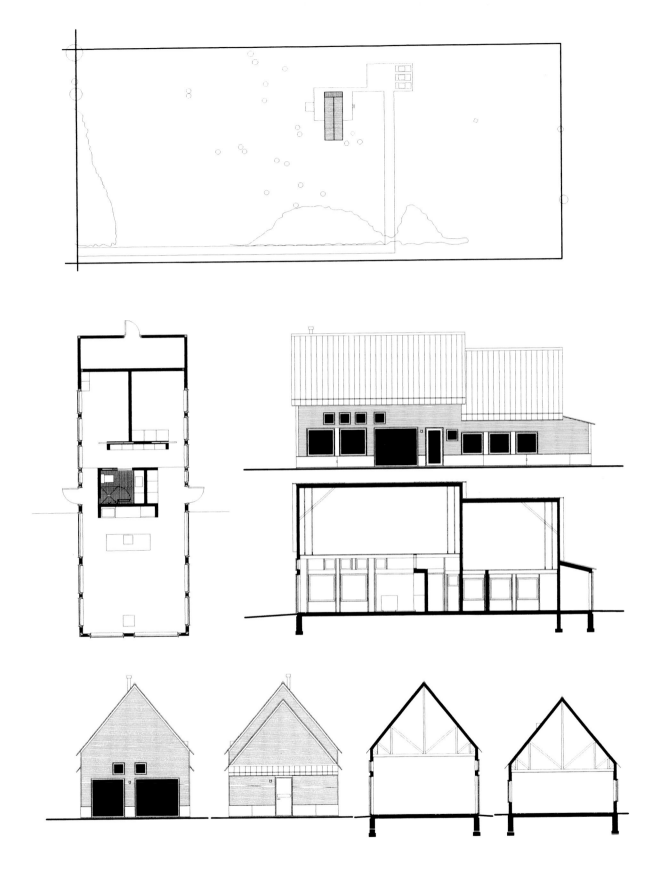

A central utility core of bathrooms and kitchen stands
in the middle of the cabin, separating the rear bedrooms
from the front living and dining space.

JORGENSON SUNDQUIST HOUSE

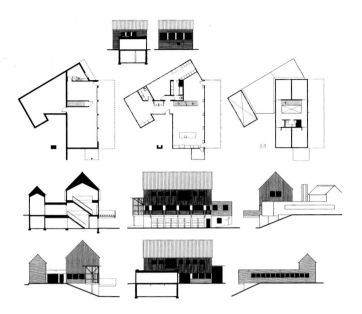

DOWNSIZING

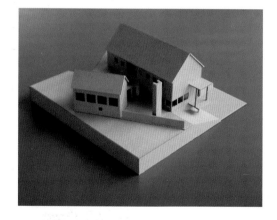

top: Enclosing an outdoor courtyard, complete with an exterior chimney, the house and music room in the original plan seem to embrace visitors.

above: The original design had a gabled music room separated from the main two-story house by an entry and master bedroom suite.

"It's human nature," says David Salmela, "that we want too much, when we can probably all live comfortably for about one-third less than we think." The house Salmela designed for the Jorgenson Sundquist family shows how an ideal design can come down in size by about one-third and still remain very livable. The original design called for a tall gable-roofed music room and flat-roofed master-bedroom suite in a one-story wing, embracing an entrance court and angled to fit the setback requirements of the tight site. That wing attached to the main three-story house, which had a three-car garage and large basement on the lower level, a living/dining/kitchen space extending the entire length of the main level, and four bedrooms on the upper floor. A screened porch supported on a single column projected off the kitchen, while a cantilevered deck running the length of the living/dining space overlooked the wetland and Lake Minnetonka in the distance. The family ended up building the three-story core of the house, minus the music and master-bedroom wing. The project was scaled down "for cost but also for sustainability reasons," says Salmela. "It's possible to live with less and still have a very nice house that exceeds people's expectations." This is what architects do, adds Salmela. "We don't try to win awards; we solve real problems."

The scaled-back version of the house that ultimately
was built simplified the form and removed the separate
music room.

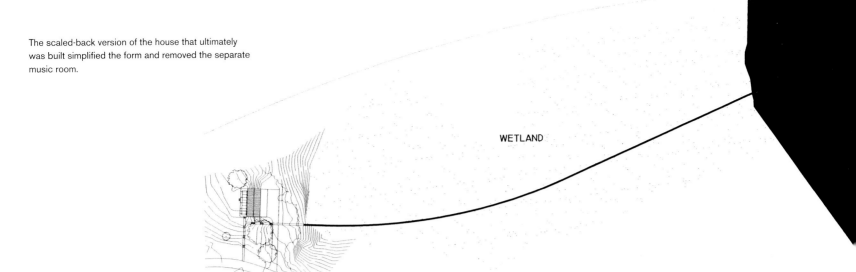

WETLAND

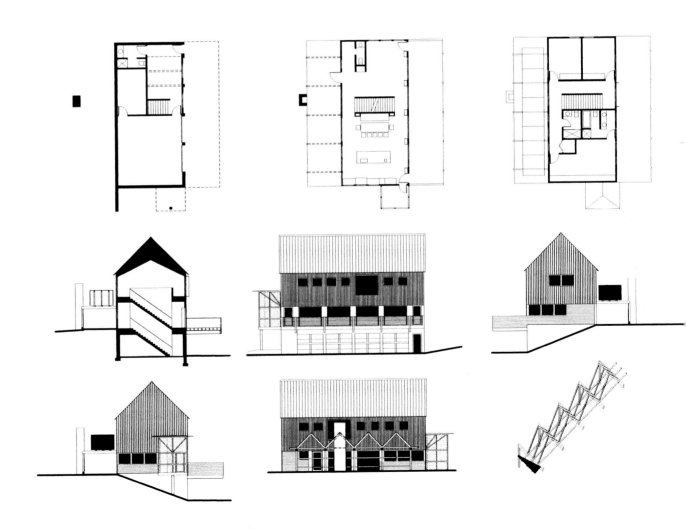

RURAL GEOMETRY

opposite: The exterior looks like a barn, with repetitive windows and batten siding, while the interior has a modern plan with spaces flowing into each other.

Farmers do more than cultivate the land; they geometrize it, creating ordered open space and rectangles of regularity amidst the undulating and irregular natural landscape. David Salmela emphasizes that fact in his vision for this house on a farm near the development he designed, Jackson Meadow. The house takes many of the same contextual cues as Jackson Meadows does from the town of Marine on St. Croix, with its numerous small, narrow, white-painted structures. The house stands at the southern end of an open space, between an existing barn and residence. A pergola on the south side of the gable-roofed house leads to a pair of glass entry doors, which gives access to the largely open first floor, with a single living/dining/kitchen space flanked by a screened porch on one side and a straight-run stair on the other. Two terraces, each with its own outdoor chimney, help extend the house into the landscape, fitting for its farm location. Upstairs, a master bedroom suite and two smaller bedrooms and another bathroom have views of open space to the north through a row of windows running the entire length of the house. The batten siding and shingled roof, echoed in a row of three outbuildings to the rear, as well as the square windows that repeat throughout the house, all reinforce the large-scale geometry of the whole.

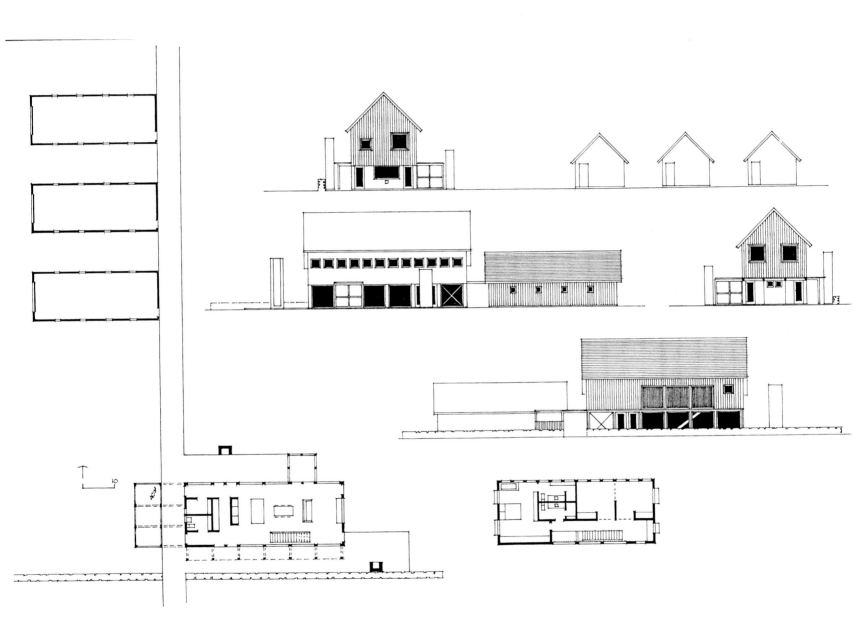

WINDBREAKS

GOLOB FREEMAN CABIN

LA POINTE, WISCONSIN

STRANGELY FAMILIAR

David Salmela does what all good artists should: render the familiar strange. To some, that may sound like an odd role for artists; the world can seem strange enough without creative people making it even more so. But art has always played that critical function in society by helping us see the ordinary things around us in new ways, if for no other reason than to have us notice them again. That becomes particularly important in an era like ours, in which creativity and innovation have become key to competing in a global economy. Art becomes a major way of overturning our assumptions and uncovering new possibilities in what we have become blind to, and in so doing, it has emerged as a critical factor in our achieving economic prosperity as well as in our having a higher quality of life in the future.

Architecture, of course, has other roles to play, such as providing functional space for people's daily lives. And its visibility to passersby, as one of the most public of the arts, also makes it more difficult for architects to engage in this "strange making" activity. If we don't like a painting, we can simply stop visiting it in a museum, but a neighbor's building we dislike becomes much harder to avoid. And yet, that also makes architecture the most powerful of the arts in helping us see things anew. Its unavoidable qualities ensure its effectiveness in stimulating the new ideas that a society needs in order to evolve.

One of the most powerful houses Salmela has done in this regard is the cabin he designed for Bruce Golob and Jean Freeman, in La Pointe, Wisconsin, on Madeline Island. You arrive at the cabin down a long drive, and so its somewhat startling quality does not intrude on neighbors, although it seems that, on tiny Madeline Island, a lot of people have seen the cabin, which has

top: The cabin stands at the end of a field, two black boxes after a white walk that terminates in a totemlike white outdoor chimney.

bottom: The high sidewalls protect the house from the wind off Lake Superior, while the screened porch and terrace are outdoor living spaces in summer.

been aptly called "two black sheds." The idea of a cabin emulating a shed seems fitting for this resort community of mostly small vacation houses. But the black color and boxlike forms set the two sheds apart from the mostly white, gable-roofed cabins in the area and fit well with the owners'—and the architect's—wry sense of humor. When Bruce Golob and Jean Freeman stand, arm in arm, smiling and waving in unison in front of their two black sheds, they seem perfect for each other.

The 900-square-foot main cabin contains a bedroom, bathroom, and kitchen/dining/living area, while the separate 360-square-foot guest cottage has a bedroom, bathroom, and storage room. The large windows and raised sidewalls hide the low-sloped gabled roofs and give the two buildings a familiar modernist feel, and yet their black color inverts our expectation of modern houses' being white. At the same time, these two strange structures bring to mind familiar images, such as the tar-papered cabins you sometimes see in the North Woods, or the traditional, blackened-log houses of Scandinavia, a part of the world that Salmela alludes to repeatedly in his work. The two black cabins also refer to the "long black ore ships that occasionally enter the channel below the site," Salmela explains: familiar objects in a strange location.

below: A dark and somewhat mysterious object, the cabin offers many opportunities to enjoy nature through its large windows and ample porch.

His playful mix of the familiar and strange continues in the patio between the two cabins. Sited by landscape architect Shane Coen to align with a point of land across the inlet, the approach walk, flanked by two light stanchions, has a grandeur that seems strange for such a narrow slip of concrete. At the same time, the walk cuts through a front yard of tall grass, a familiar space treated in an unexpected way. The walk leads to a terrace that separates the two buildings, centered on an "unchimney" as Salmela calls it: a three-sided, white-painted brick flue against which logs burn, as if the front of the chimney had been inexplicably removed. Meanwhile, in a play on the abandoned sofas that sometimes populate the porches of backwoods houses, Salmela has furnished the patio with a bright-green plastic sofa designed by Philippe Starck, a familiar form that looks oddly out of place, as if part of the house had blown away, leaving the living room sofa untouched.

The clients, a retired schoolteacher and a management consultant from the Twin Cities, love this play on people's expectations. "This was not our initial vision," says Jean Freeman, "but when David showed us the sketches and talked about possible exterior colors, including black, we immediately said 'black.' The same happened with the plastic couch. When he suggested it and recommended that it be lime green, we instantly said yes. The color seems natural, like the color of early spring leaves." Salmela likens the two black cabins to another form of nature. "They're like two barking dogs," he jests, "that want you to come up and pet them." As if to bark back at nature, Salmela has also put a lightly framed screened porch outside the north-facing wall, with a butterfly roof that sheds the rain, like a big scupper, spouting back to Lake Superior whatever wind and water it sends this way.

The sense of strangeness and familiarity occurs on the cabins' interiors as well. Unlike the basic-black exterior, the insides of the cabins are all color and light. "David originally talked about the interior having white walls, birch cabinets, and an ochre-color ceiling," says Freeman, "but I had a deep-red handbag whose color we liked, so David had the painters match its color for

above: The screened porch has an inverted V-shaped roof that sheds rain while opening up the view on either side to the sky and surrounding trees.

right: The open plan and simple elevations recall the straightforward and uncomplicated quality that once characterized cabin culture.

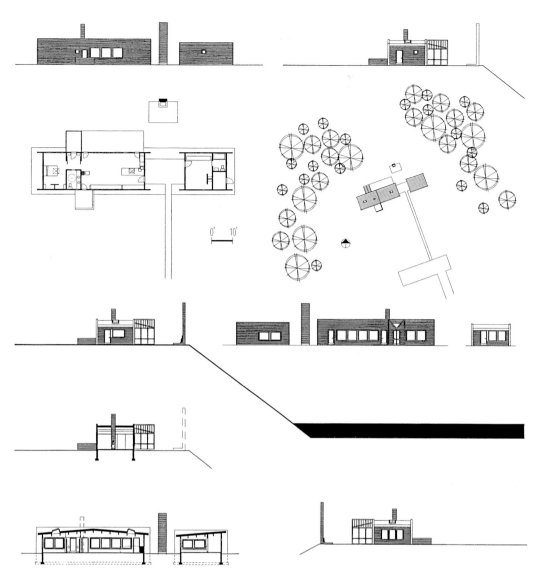

the concrete floors. And once he saw that, he said that the cabinets had to be Italian violet. He was right." While unfamiliar, those colors coat familiar cabin materials: flush pine-board walls, stressed-skin plywood ceilings, and glulam beams spanning the eighteen-foot-wide spaces. Adding to the warmth of the interior is the sun, which pours through two skylights and large, square, awning windows, while at night, low-voltage lights strung on cables between the beams make the floor and ceiling glow.

David Salmela plays, in this modest project, with our expectations of what a cabin should be. On one hand, it lives up to what we expect in such structures: simple materials, durable surfaces, and unpretentious spaces. On the other hand, Salmela makes the familiar strange, giving us two cabins where we anticipate one, a black exterior when we expect white, colorful interiors instead of natural ones, modern forms rather than traditional ones. This has resulted in something both strange and strangely familiar, a cabin that not only comfortably accommodates its owners on vacation but also offers them and their friends and neighbors an ongoing holiday from their preconceptions, and that might be the best break of all.

above: In contrast to the dark exterior, the inside of the cabin features bright colors: a red floor, a yellow ceiling, and violet cabinets in a white enclosure.

right: The large windows along both sides of the narrow cabin fill the interior with light, aided by the open plan and painted wood walls.

CLIENT CONFIDENCE

Unlike most of the other arts, in which artists largely generate their own work for eventual presentation, publication, or performance, architecture follows a more complicated route toward completion. An architect must seek commissions from clients and work with them as well as myriad others, ranging from consultants and code officials to contractors and community members, to get a building constructed. The skill in navigating this maze matters as much as the talent of the architect in design and detailing, but even those architects most adept at this process cannot succeed without the support of good clients.

Evidence of the difference good clients can make lies here, in this "cabin" that architect David Salmela and landscape architect Shane Coen designed for David and Kathy Matthew on Gull Lake in northern Minnesota. The Matthews had long admired Salmela's work, and when their previous cabin burned to the ground, they pursued Salmela to design them a new one. "I was really busy," says Salmela, "but they kept calling, and one day, I found them sitting on the bench outside my office. They were so delightful and so determined, how could I say no?"

The original cabin stood parallel to the lake, but "the first time I saw the site," says Salmela, "I realized that they would get more of a view if the cabin stood perpendicular to the water. Being in a summer cabin is wonderful, and you want to enjoy it all day, eating breakfast in the morning sun, watching the sunset in the evening. The plan of the house fell into place after that."

A long, narrow garage fronts the road, pushed to one side of the site to avoid a grove of mature trees. "A double garage would have overwhelmed the front of the lot, so we stacked the cars,

top: Viewed across a front yard of wildflowers, the complex echoes the pattern of neighboring cabins, with garage in front and house toward the lake.

above: A walk extends along the garage's wood sidewall toward a slot of space that gives a tantalizing view of the lake beyond the house.

one behind the other," explains Salmela. Behind the garage stands a separate sauna, guest room, and mechanical and storage building, necessary because the site's high water table precluded a basement.

The twenty-by-fifty-six-foot, two-story house stands in a swath of lush native grass that extends from the road to the lake. "The landscape has a rural feeling," says Salmela, "that helps the cabin fit its surroundings." Wide bluestone terraces, enclosed by white-painted trellises and wood-slat fences, extend along both sides of the house, expanding the largely glazed living spaces on the first floor out toward the edges of the narrow site.

The Matthews understood and appreciated Salmela's minimalist aesthetic. "The house is like a canvas," says Kathy Matthew, referring to the two-story, white-painted concrete-block facade, whose nearly blank south-facing surface captures the ever-changing patterns of the surrounding trees. Meanwhile, the multiple reflections in the house's large sheets of glass appeal to David Matthew. "You see reflections of the lake as you look into the house and out a far window to another view of the lake," he explains.

Visually tying the garage, house, and sauna together, the white masonry end walls have an abstract quality that also affords privacy from the street.

The clients supported that same sensibility in the landscape. To get visitors to the front door on the far side of the house, "I thought a diagonal walk made sense," says Kathy Matthew, but there was no other diagonal in the house. Shane Coen instead orchestrated an orthogonal alternative. He ran a narrow bluestone walk between the garage and the front yard of native grass, past a stone wall that prevents people from walking onto the back terrace, down some steps to a turf-grass lawn, and along a stone retaining wall to the front terrace, where the lake finally comes into view. That elegant entry sequence, along with the various fences that line both sides of the lot, "has given us privacy from the neighbors that we never had before," says Kathy Matthew.

Meanwhile, the house's interior, says David Matthew, has "an almost organic quality, with what seems like the right amount of space, whether it's just the two of us, or a party of eighty people."

Visitors enter the house from a side stone-paved terrace that is covered by a white-painted trellis and screened from the neighbors by a white picket fence.

That comes, in part, from Salmela's skill at structuring interior space. The living-dining-kitchen-study occupies a single room extending the entire length of the house. The only divisions in that room are a fireplace along an exterior wall, a stair enclosure of white wood slats, and an enclosed toilet/laundry room area, all of which break down the scale of the space and indicate where furniture might go.

Upstairs, a hallway opens out to the living spaces below, with a library nook at one end and a screened porch at the other. A line of windows illuminates the eight-foot-wide upper hall, with the openings gradually widening toward the view of the lake. Three bedrooms and two bathrooms on the second floor face west, with angled windows that provide views of the lake and capture some of the southern sun. "The angled windows open out to the sound and the breeze from the lake," says Salmela, "giving the house a more casual feeling."

Because of the visual activity along the sides of the house and outbuildings—extensive trellises, angled bays, windows of various sizes—Salmela felt the need to control it with the end walls: white masonry planes that extend beyond the side walls and above the low-sloped roofs of all three structures. "There was a lot happening in the midzone of the buildings," he says, "so I wanted to make the ends minimal, to balance it all."

Those minimalist, billboardlike elements proved to be one of the most controversial parts of the project. "The community tried to stop the project more than once," says David Matthew. "One neighbor saw the block walls going up and said that we were building a Target store." But the Matthews stuck by their architect. "Our relationship with David's firm was built on trust," says Kathy Matthew. "We wanted to do something significant, and we got what we wanted, a bold, but very warm and welcoming house." "Even the neighbors like it now," adds her husband.

"This is what art is supposed to do," says Kathy Matthew, an art history major in college. "The house has gotten people talking and questioning what they assume to be the right thing to do." That questioning even applies to the designers themselves. "The cabin is different from what the Matthews thought they'd get," says Salmela, with a chuckle, "and it is also different from what I thought they'd get." But if you ask David and Kathy Matthew, they know exactly what they got. "In the business book *Good to Great,*" says David Matthew, "the great CEOs are humble people who have a strong vision. That is definitely true of David Salmela." It is also true of the Matthews: good clients whose humility and vision led them to support great work.

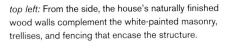

top left: From the side, the house's naturally finished wood walls complement the white-painted masonry, trellises, and fencing that encase the structure.

top right: A wall of full-height windows and glass doors offers a view into the house, with its white staircase and wood-slat screen glowing in the light.

bottom left: Inside the entry hall, visitors see past the stairs of the living/dining/kitchen space, whose wood ceiling draws the eye out to the view.

bottom right: An oriental carpet over the slate floor defines the living area, which receives light from its large windows and the clerestory along the second floor.

top: By pulling the second level back from the wall, Salmela creates a slot of space that makes the main level feel larger and gives it more light.

bottom: On the second, bedroom level, the wood floor echoes the wood ceiling and visually warms the rooms, which look out to the canopy of surrounding trees.

top: The angled side windows, the second-story screened porch, and the trellised terraces all take maximum advantage of the house's lakeside location.

bottom: The plan shows how the house, garage, and sauna utilize the entire site, which has been arranged to provide visual privacy for the extensive outdoor space.

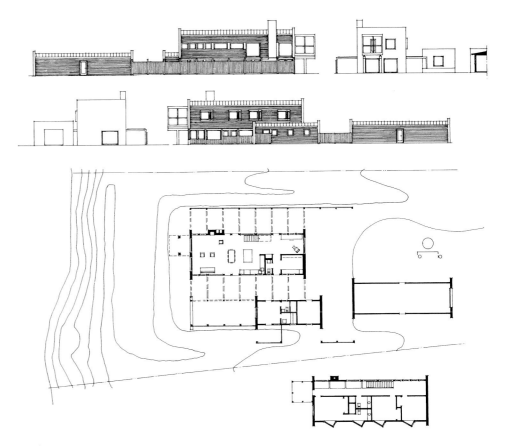

THE USES OF ENCHANTMENT

In his book *The Uses of Enchantment,* the psychologist Bruno Bettelheim writes about how fairy tales help children understand the world around them, with nature and architecture playing particularly important roles in several stories. "Since ancient times," writes Bettelheim, "the near impenetrable forest . . . has symbolized the dark, hidden . . . world of our unconscious" from which we "emerge with a much more highly developed humanity," as happens with Little Red Riding Hood and Hansel and Gretel. At the same time, whether it is the gingerbread house that the witch uses to lure little children, or the houses of straw, sticks, and brick that the three little pigs build as protection against the big, bad wolf, dwellings have represented, in fairy tales, our maturation as individuals and as a species.

"Play reaches the habits most needed for intellectual growth," wrote Bettelheim, and the same could be said for the serious play that constitutes design, with its imaginative transformation of ordinary reality into something psychologically satisfying and personally memorable. An example of this is the retreat that David Salmela has designed for doctors Douglas and Bonnie Yingst of Detroit. The house's heavily wooded lakeside site west of Traverse City, Michigan, has a mysterious quality reminiscent of a fairy tale forest. "The tall beech trees give the site a quiet, moody quality," says Salmela. And the house and its outbuildings so thoroughly play upon our expectations of what such buildings should look like that they entice you to enter and explore, as happens so often in the tales of our childhood. "It's so relaxing here," says Bonnie Yingst. "We hate to leave it."

You arrive at the property by traversing a long drive through the forest, coming to a gravel auto court fronted by four, separate, black-clad structures set in a row, with the tallest one standing

Standing deep in the forest, the black outbuildings and the white-walled house have an uncertain scale, looking large and small at the same time.

opposite, top to bottom: The black Skatelite-clad garages and the white-painted masonry facade of the house look like chess pieces ready for play on a board of grass and gravel.

From the side, the house looks accordion-like, with wood columns, dark windows, and black Skatelite walls expanded out between the white end walls.

The black garages on a gravel drive seem like sentries guarding the main house beyond, with narrow passageways leading into the compound.

The land steps down toward the lake, with stairs and a retaining wall at the end of a terrace that is partly covered by the wood trellis along the side of the house.

slightly askew. While these black masses serve the prosaic functions of garage, workshop, and guest room, you feel like the wanderer in a fairy tale, finding something strange in the woods and wondering what these oddly silent structures could be. Beyond them beckons the house, its tall white end wall standing in stark contrast to the buildings before you, and you have almost no choice but to follow the concrete path that leads you between the black masses to the seemingly magical landscape beyond.

Salmela likens the garages to "pieces of black cheese" and the adjacent house, with its white masonry facade and repetitive, exterior, glulam columns set off against black, Skatelite-clad sidewalls, to "a sliced loaf of dark bread." That culinary analogy continues in his design of the site immediately around the house. "We treated the landscape like a table," says Salmela, "with sidewalks that project above the ground," making the areas of gravel, grass, and crushed slate that surround the house feel like enormous place mats, with the narrow concrete walks providing a place for us to pass between them. The sense you get of having walked onto a table set for a giant's feast or game of chess gives the landscape a fablelike quality unlike anything you have ever encountered.

In fables, of course, things are never what they seem, and the same is true of the Yingst retreat. Off in the woods stands one of the most peculiar and intriguing structures Salmela has yet to design: what looks like a giant black caterpillar making its way among the trees to the lake. With its head lifted up, as if on alert for a possible predator, the structure has a kinked back, as if poised to continue crawling once the coast is clear, seeming to be in no more of a hurry than the hookah-smoking caterpillar that Alice comes upon in her *Adventures in Wonderland.* When you approach it, you discover its true purpose: an open pavilion providing shelter from the rain and a place in which to sleep on a warm summer night. Indeed, the bed in the middle of the pavilion, shrouded in mosquito netting, has a ghostly presence, like a soul hovering mysteriously in the belly of this black-bug building.

Salmela seems equally mysterious when he talks about the structure. "There needed to be a place to sit out among the trees," he said, giving no explanation for the fantastic form itself. "The original design was too expensive and difficult to build," he adds, "so we found a way to simplify it." And there it stands, two irregular timber trusses, tilted against each other and standing on

The wood trellis shelters the entry walk that extends from the front yard, beside a bed of crushed slate, to the slate-paved terrace by the front door.

top: Inside the entry, a stair with a wood-slat screen ascends to the second floor, while the slate floor leads visitors around the fireplace to the living room.

bottom: The kitchen and adjoining dining area stand several steps below the entry level, with an office beyond the kitchen, a few steps farther down the slope.

top: Placed in a two-story space, with the balcony overlooking it, the dining room table becomes a central gathering point in the house.

bottom: Viewed from the lowest level, the cascading slate-covered stairs rise to the living room and master bedroom at the far end of the house.

opposite: Large glulam beams span the width of the house, creating a consistent rhythm and a uniform datum as the main floor steps down.

six legs on a concrete pad, with a zigzag roof covering the structure and keeping out the rain. It begs you to demand, as the caterpillar did of Alice, "Explain yourself!" to which Alice responded, "I can't explain MYSELF." Nor can this caterpillar-like construction explain itself: it stands there so wonderfully magical that it needs no other explanation.

A similar Alice-in-Wonderland experience occurs as you face the house itself. Like the face of the Cheshire Cat that appears suddenly among the branches, the facade has a pair of small windows like two eyes to the side above a large, glassy projecting "mouth" topped by a grass roof "mustache." This gives the house an expression of pleasant surprise, as if it's happy to see an unexpected visitor. The sidewalls of the house, whose tall wood columns recall the "trees in the surrounding woods," says Douglas Yingst, entice you to follow them to the front door, under the long covered colonnade, whose repetitive glulam beams and columns that extend along one side of the house seem to come right out of Lewis Carroll's imagination. It feels like an enchanted tunnel in which you leave the familiar world behind to come upon a door through which you will enter into yet another magical place.

And so you do when you cross the threshold of the Yingst retreat. Contrary to the mostly black exterior, the inside has light-colored walls, slate-tile floors that offer a more orderly version of the crushed slate outside, and exposed wood columns and beams that represent an enlarged version of the colonnade outside. Here, rather than feeling like a small intruder in a big table setting, you have a sense of everything being exactly the right size. The closed, boxlike exterior gives way to the largely open, flowing interior that cascades down the hill in a series of levels in what seems like one large room.

You enter at a midlevel into a warm, wood-lined entry hall, with wood-slatted stairs that lead up to guest bedrooms and recreation space on the mezzanine above. Straight ahead, you come to a wide hall that connects the living area and master bedroom suite to your left and the kitchen and dining area down several stairs to your right. A white-painted masonry mass stands like a sentinel, protecting the living room from the entry and providing a backdrop for the fireplace and flat-screen television. A series of partitions, with pocket doors for closures, divide the living room from the bathroom/laundry room suite and the master bedroom beyond.

Continuing to your right, down a half level, you discover an expansive kitchen with capacity for two cooks at the same time, and a dining table beneath a row of suspended white light fixtures. Down another half flight stands the study, overlooking the lake, with another set of stairs leading to a basement. The long, two-story, window-lined space that ties all these spaces together also visually links the interior back to the forest outside, with its white-painted outdoor fireplace, grass-roofed sauna, and caterpillar-like pavilion. "You constantly feel drawn outside with all the windows," observes Bonnie Yingst.

"The cleverness of the house," adds her husband, "is that, despite the openness inside and out, each space feels intimate and just the right scale." Salmela attributes that to the way the house reacts to the sloping site. "You enter from the side into a low space," he says, "and the house opens up both vertically and lengthwise as you move through it." As Alice kept discovering in

top: The white-painted masonry fireplace and adjoining television screen are focal points in the living room as well as sculptural forms in the house.

bottom: The master bathroom and bedroom look out to the side yard and retain visual privacy from the bedrooms above with a high horizontal-slat railing.

above: Two-story walls of glass along the main circulation route bring ample light into the interior as well as broad views of the surrounding forest.

right: Upstairs, the bedrooms and recreation space have skylights and also windows along both sides, which make the narrow mezzanine seem large.

Wonderland, you feel smaller and then larger as you move toward and then through the house. Bettelheim writes that "for a story . . . to hold a child's attention, it must entertain him and arouse his curiosity . . . enrich his life . . . stimulate his imagination . . . develop his intellect and . . . clarify his emotions." Those same characteristics apply to the Yingst retreat. It, too, holds your attention by arousing curiosity and stimulating the imagination in both intellectual and emotional ways. How he does it, Salmela won't tell: "I can't really define it," he says. But then neither can we ever quite define the power of fairy tales and why they remain with us into adulthood. That's their enchantment.

below: The rear of the house has an asymmetrical composition of windows in its white masonry end wall, echoed in the white-painted masonry fireplace.

right: The site plan shows how the main house projects toward the lake, flanked by garages on one side and the sauna and pavilion on the other.

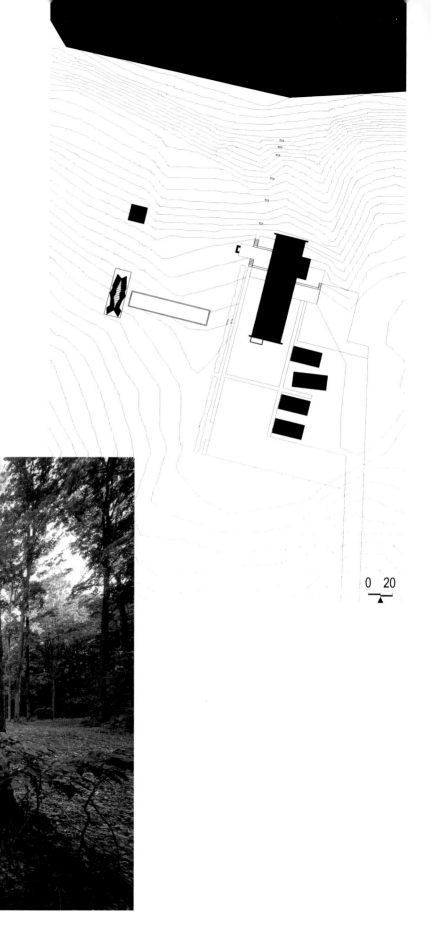

0 20

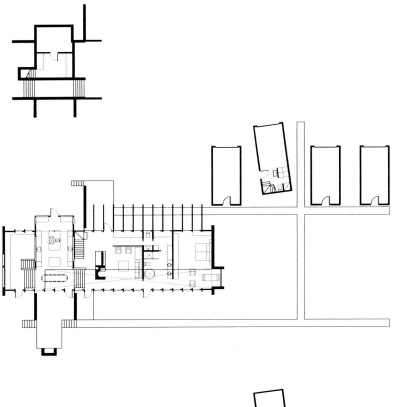

left: Within the regular rhythm of the glulam columns and beams, the house has an open plan, with spaces flowing into or overlooking each other.

below: A wide variety of window placements furnishes a backdrop for the highly irregular form of the nearby pavilion.

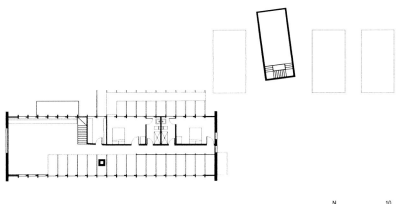

N   10

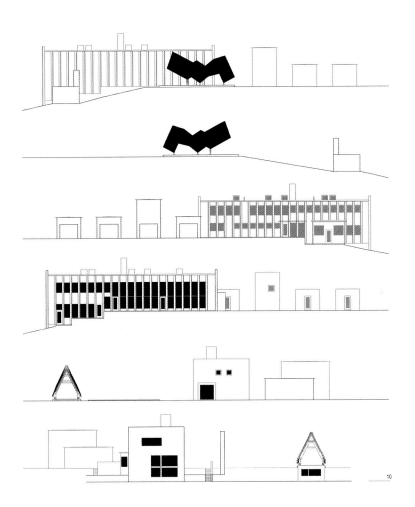

10

top to bottom: Outside the dining area are a terrace and outdoor chimney, with a white-painted stand-alone sauna and the black-painted pavilion in the distance.

Mosquito netting protects from bugs in the summer and lends an almost eerie quality to the pavilion, glowing white in the darkness.

The jagged form of the pavilion looks like a piece of minimalist sculpture or an odd creature inching toward the sauna before it jumps in the lake.

Composed of two irregular wood trusses tilted up against each other, the pavilion is an airy space at once sheltering and spirited.

The buglike pavilion offers a covered place to sit in
the woods and to watch games of bocce ball played
in the adjacent court.

SCHIFMAN HOUSE

MINNEAPOLIS, MINNESOTA

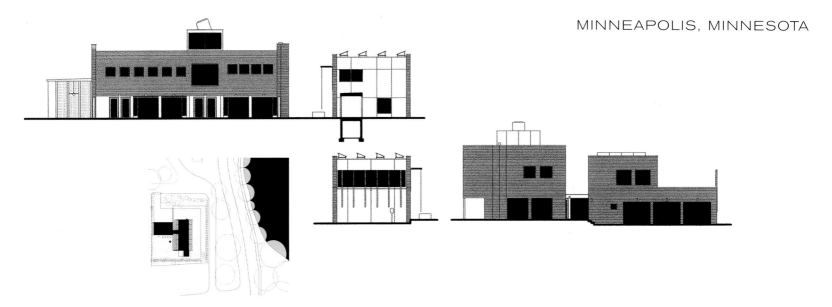

DRAMA ON THE LAKE

top: The tall end walls of the house provide privacy on its corner urban lot, while the landscape offers extensive outdoor space enclosed by planted borders.

above: Shielded from the road by a row of arborvitae, the house has a wood-clad upper floor from which the Schifmans can view the neighboring lake.

The Schifmans hired David Salmela to design a house at a prime corner overlooking Cedar Lake in Minneapolis, where most water frontage remains public. Lissie Schifman also had ambitious environmental goals for the house, wanting it to demonstrate LEED principles. Salmela, along with landscape architect Shane Coen, handled the conflict between lake view and privacy by lining the Schifmans' lot with arborvitae, a thick, coniferous shrub. Salmela then maximized water views as well as passive solar heating with glass walls along the main floor living room, entry hall, dining room, and kitchen and with rows of square windows along the second-floor bedrooms and stair hall. Salmela further controlled views by locating the three-car garage wing perpendicular to the house to shield the backyard from neighbors. And he planted green roofs over the garage and entry hall to offer a pleasant perspective from the upstairs office and bedrooms. The house uses frugal materials: recycled cypress, dark brick, and stucco. But it has a spacious generosity, with tall ceilings, large windows, and a broad, central stair hall, with an operable skylight that can cool the entire house. As in many Salmela houses, the simple, open plan of the Schifmans' house does not convey its richness. "The place is powerful," says Salmela, "and the spaces are dramatic." And the views of Cedar Lake? Priceless.

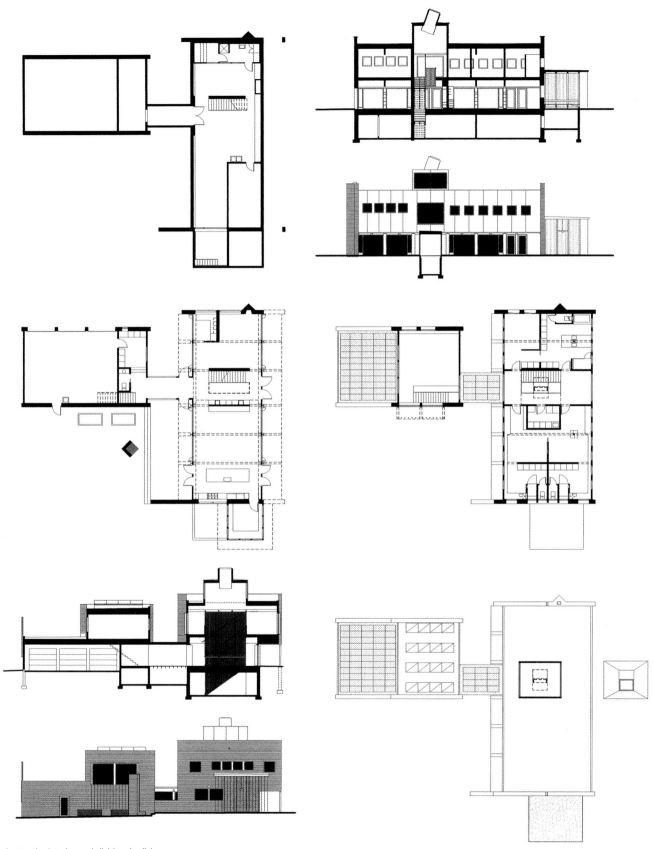

A skylit stairwell illuminates the interior and divides the living
room from the kitchen/dining room and the bedrooms above.

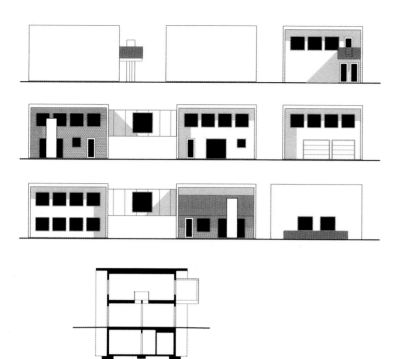

ODEH HOUSE

ROCHESTER, MINNESOTA

OUT OF THE BOX

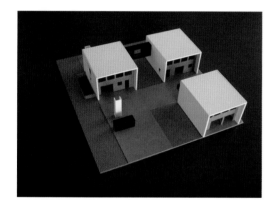

top: With nearly blank sidewalls, the house's front and rear elevations feature large windows to take advantage of the views in the wooded lot.

above: The three-part house has a front garage with guest quarters above and a bedroom box linked by a bridge to the main living spaces.

This house, intended for a radiologist and his family in Rochester, explores the "prairie house" idea David Salmela evolved as part of the Mayo Woodlands development he designed with landscape architect Shane Coen. Envisioned as a collection of open-ended concrete enclosures, the house, says Salmela, is "like three Donald Judd boxes." The front box contains a two-car garage, with a stair up to an in-law apartment above it, all contained within the insulated concrete shell that rises up and over the wood-framed infill of doors, windows, and walls. The two boxes behind it contain the main living spaces, with a second-story bridge connecting the two structures. The box on the left encloses the kitchen, living, and dining spaces on the main floor, with a stair leading up to a play space and two small offices, and a stair leading down to a recreational space and a bathroom and sauna in the basement, looking out to a recessed court. The box on the right, behind the garage, houses two bedrooms and a bathroom on the first floor, with a stair leading up to a master bedroom suite on the second. By distributing a typical house into these three boxes, Salmela helps us see the different aspects of family life as a set of discrete experiences, in a completely out-of-the-box way.

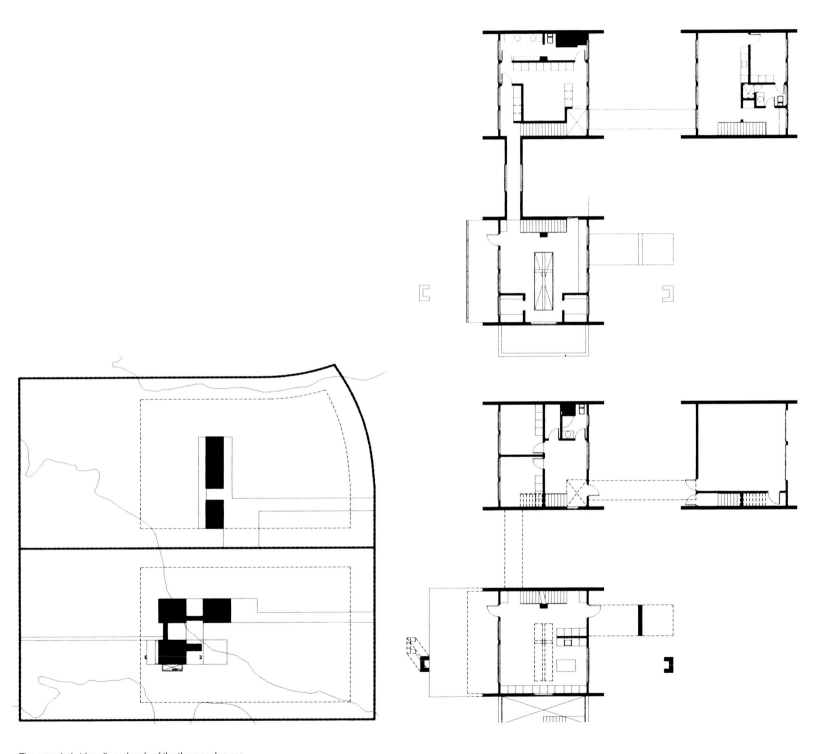

The extended sidewalls and roofs of the three enclosures
shield the house from neighbors and protect the wood-clad
infill walls from the elements.

SHEDS

REDUCING OUR FOOTPRINT

We hear a lot these days about our ecological footprint, a term that describes the often-negative impact humans have on the planet. At current levels of consumption, our footprint has outgrown the globe, which makes reducing our use of resources and lowering our generation of greenhouse gases so urgent. This can seem an overwhelming issue for most of us, since we depend on technology that contributes to the problem (gas-powered cars, jet-fueled airplanes, coal-fired power plants) with relatively few alternatives. That may change, of course. Electric cars, electric trains, wind turbines, and a host of other innovations have become more common and more readily available to those of us who want to help reduce our planetary footprint. But there is something else we can all do right now that would have a much faster and greater effect than all the new green technology combined: living with less.

Reducing our demands may seem an onerous task, bringing to mind for some the specter of shivering in some small, dark place. But the cabin compound that David Salmela designed for Chris and Helen Roland on Wisconsin's Madeline Island offers insight into how we might reduce our ecological footprint and live with less while also increasing the richness, lowering the stress, and enhancing the quality of our lives. The first step in lessening our impact involves reusing whatever we can—and that is exactly what Chris and Helen Roland did when they purchased a heavily wooded site on Madeline Island, overlooking Lake Superior and the Wisconsin mainland. The land contained a cabin the original owners had built themselves. "It stood on log stumps," says Chris Roland, "and was falling apart, and we knew we had to rebuild it. We had read about David Salmela, and we knew he did small houses, but when we saw the Golob Freeman cabin on the island, we knew he was our architect."

top to bottom: The black-clad buildings stand in a mature forest, with a garage and guesthouse on one side of a shallow ravine and the sauna and main house on the other.

A small bridge spans the ravine, giving guests in the cabin to the left access to the sauna and the main house to the right, which is closer to the water.

The sauna's bright checkerboard door gives the small structure a playful quality appropriate to its purpose, echoing the form and material of the guesthouse.

The zoning laws had changed since the original cabin was built, however, and the Rolands were no longer allowed to build so close to the shore of the lake. This restriction required, says David Salmela, that "we use the same footprint as the existing cabin, and reuse as many of its materials as possible, in order to meet the letter of the law." He adds, "It's like obeying the speed limit. You can break it when passing another car, but if you go too fast all the time, you'll get caught. We didn't tear anything totally down in the main cabin so that it could be considered a major remodeling." The environmental as well as the economic benefits of such an approach show how communities can, through a tool like zoning, encourage us to be more creative in rethinking what exists. "It's harder to build within an existing footprint," admits Salmela, "but the best design comes from constraints, and so it was good that we had those limits to work within."

Because they were required to stay within the small footprint of the original cabin, the Rolands purchased the adjacent wooded lot that had no building on it, commissioning Salmela to design a guest cabin, as well as a garage and sauna, farther back from the lakeshore, as zoning required. Although this enlarged the size of the Rolands' cabin, it allowed Salmela to reduce

top to bottom: Large windows in the main cabin face back toward the forest and offer an alternative view to the dominant vista of Lake Superior in the other direction.

Its small footprint and dark color help the main cabin disappear in the shade of the forest so that it does not visually disrupt the island's pristine shoreline.

Sitting in the tall screened porch, you feel like you are outdoors—a sensation enhanced by the skylights that illuminate the porch and let light into the cabin.

above: In contrast to the black exterior, light fills the main cabin's interior through its spacious windows, ample skylights, and large suspended light fixtures.

right: The sloped ceiling rises from a one-story height on the forest side to a two-story screened porch, which makes the small cabin interior feel much larger.

opposite: Large operable windows allow cross ventilation through the main cabin and turn the screened porch into an extension of the living room inside.

the compound's ecological footprint in another way. "We located the guest cabin, garage, and sauna to minimize the removal of vegetation," he explains, "disturbing the land as little as possible, with native plants to fill in the gaps." Given the carbon-sequestering role that plant life plays, Salmela's locating of buildings among the trees becomes not just a cost-effective and aesthetically pleasing strategy but also the most environmentally responsible one.

The structures, scattered among the trees, also seem to have arisen over a long period of time, as if having served some original purpose as a campground. Small design details reinforce that quality. The thin ribbons of concrete that lead from the garage to the guest cabin, across a bridge over the ravine, past the sauna, and to the main cabin look as if they cover earlier paths that had emerged from years of use. Likewise, flat wide boards around entrances have the appearance of additions attached at a later point, as if to enhance the place. "Architecture," says Salmela, "should be almost subliminal, affecting us without our being fully aware of it."

The notion that these new structures remind us of something very old continues in their several sustainable features. Clad in black Skatelite panels made of recycled paper, the cabins also contain recycled timber frames that Salmela calls "a wiser product, without the irregularities of new wood and the twists and turns of life." Wood-clad interior walls, echoing the more rustic cabins of earlier eras, also provide durability, with a minimum of maintenance, further reducing the resources needed to live there. Ample daylight and ventilation through the cabins' large operable windows and skylights also minimize the need for artificial lighting and eliminate the need for air-conditioning. When it gets too hot, you can almost live in the main cabin's large screened porch, with its thirteen-foot-high roof and tall, cross-braced structure that echo the form of the surrounding trees. And when it's cold, you can retreat to the nearby sauna, with its recycled brick and blond wood interior.

The Rolands' compound may serve as a year-round vacation retreat, but the cabins, each approximately nine hundred square feet, seem ample enough for the kind of humble living that we will all need to embrace if we are ever to reduce our ecological footprint. They can accommodate a number of people, not only in their compact bedrooms, but also with features such as a long, built-in bench whose upholstered cushions Salmela has designed to flip over and serve as a place for several to sleep. Through their small size and placement relatively far apart, the separate structures in this complex also allow for the animal and plant life that has long occupied the site to continue thriving with minimal interruption. Salmela's design offers us not only an example of how little we really need in order to lead a comfortable, capacious existence but also an indication of what a much more modest and environmentally responsible good life might entail, after the old, unsustainable "good life" is gone.

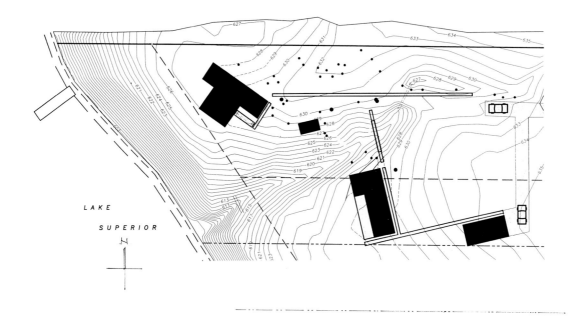

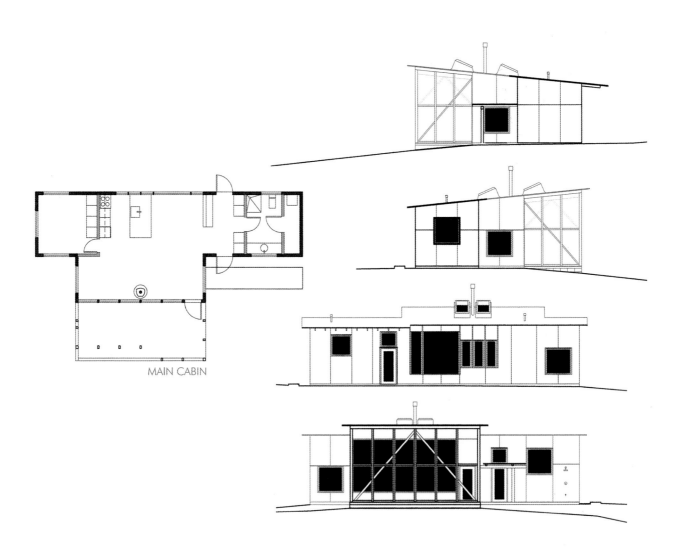

LAKE

SUPERIOR

MAIN CABIN

opposite, top to bottom: The site plan shows how the four structures remain scattered across two adjoining lots, each located to preserve the terrain and the trees.

The main cabin has a bathroom and utility core on one end and a bedroom on the other, with a living/dining/kitchen space in the middle.

this page, top to bottom: The sauna has become a Salmela signature, usually containing a dressing area and the sauna proper, with its heat source and wood-bench seating.

With two bedrooms and a bathroom in one wing, the guest-house's living area features a built-in bench that doubles as additional sleeping space.

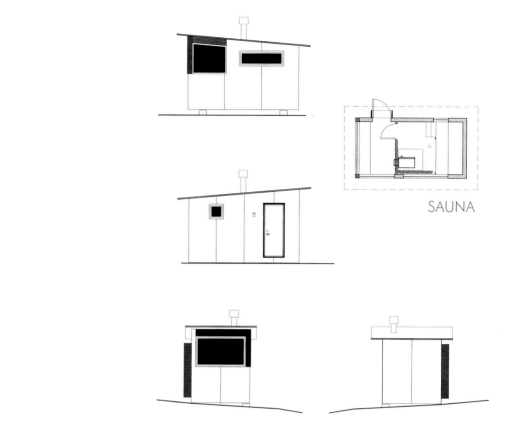

SAUNA

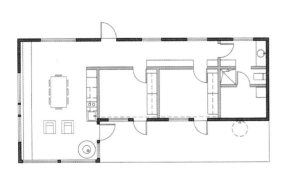

GUEST CABIN

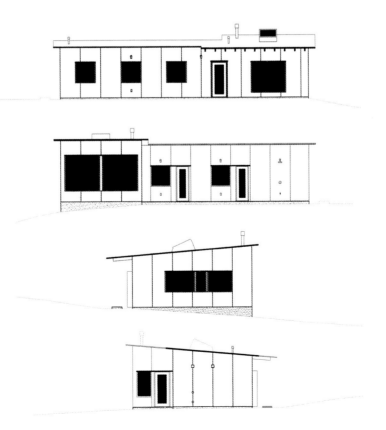

THIS WORLD SO MANY HAVE LEFT

For many years, Tom Cotruvo managed economic development for the city of Duluth, and he knows well the challenges of keeping cities vital in the wake of so many people having left urban areas for the suburbs and northern cities for warmer climates. "Tom has been great at seeing the potential of marginal sites in the city," says David Salmela. "He found the site for the Hawks Boots Factory, and he found this overlooked lot on Lake Superior, just a few miles north of downtown, for his own house." We tend to think of creativity involving the invention of something new, but the work of Tom Cotruvo and that of David Salmela in designing the Cotruvos' house show how the reimagining and repurposing of what already exists constitutes as much an innovation as anything begun from scratch.

That principle relates to cities as much as it does buildings or inventions. Many people moved to the suburbs in search of raw land upon which to build, as if a new house demanded a new site, one that had perhaps served as farmland or maybe never ceased being a forest before it became residential lots. Too many missed, in the process, the myriad ways in which the careful and creative consideration of urban land could help find new purposes or accommodate new uses for it. The last stanza of Louis Simpson's poem, "Luminous Night," might serve as a motto for all who would reinhabit our cities: "We can live here . . . this world so many have left."

You approach the Cotruvos' house down what looks, at first, like an alley off the main road that leads northeast out of Duluth along Lake Superior. Many of the large, older houses along that road had deep lots, and some owners divided their properties to create smaller sites along the shore. Tom and Christina Cotruvo found such a lot. It didn't look promising, wedged between

left: Visible between its pair of garages, this urban house has a nearly blank elevation to the street, saving its view for Lake Superior at the rear of the lot.

right: The entryway is at the side of the house, under a white trellis that faces a side yard with a planted border shielding it from the neighboring property.

other structures and behind a large house whose previous owners had once possessed the land, but as David Salmela thought when he first saw the site, "This is the way the Italians would do it." And his design follows that initial instinct, creating a beautiful, private, European-scaled compound that opens out to the lake while largely closing out the apparent chaos around it.

Salmela achieved that goal, in part, by placing a two-car garage and storage building at the front of the site and by using the slope of the land to shield most of the house and yard from the road. He also placed the house along the northern side of the site, with a heavily planted fence along the southern side to block out views of nearby structures. A row of columnar juniper trees runs along the wooden fence, with birch trees, three feet on center, in front of them, creating a colorful enclosure to the side yard. In contrast to the compressed, urban feel of the yard, the trees along the shore bring a sense of expansiveness and wildness to the site. Salmela ties the two aspects of the landscape together with a path that extends between the garage and storage building, down a set of steps, under a pergola along the side of the house and yard, and out along a grassy path to a patio and firewall that offer views up and down the lake.

The roofs of the buildings further tie the site together. The shed roof over the garage and the long roof that slopes the length of the long, narrow house have the same height and pitch. The white-painted, concrete-block garage and the naturally colored, wood-clad storage building at the front of the lot are echoed in the white block base of the house and its natural wood–clad second floor. The use of the same roof pitch and exterior materials conveys a sense of the compound having once been connected and only later becoming detached as separate structures, creating small, found spaces on the property that you discover as you move through the site, much as the site itself was discovered by moving through the city.

The idea of the city as something so many people have left carries through into the house itself. The main level of the house, with its multiple glass doors, consists essentially of one large room, with a wood screen, a kitchen island, an open stairway, and a metal fireplace that suggest the

top: The wood-clad upper level, with its small square windows, stands in contrast to the white-painted lower floor with its series of large glass doors.

middle: Facing Lake Superior, the house maximizes the view with large square windows in the master bedroom above and glass walls in the lower living room.

bottom: The garage, with its translucently glazed upper storage area, gives visual privacy to the yard, which steps down in a series of terraces to the lake.

above: Although the house stands on a narrow city lot, its location and window placement make it feel like a secluded site in the country.

bottom, left to right: Glass doors illuminate the living and dining area, where colorful modern furnishings complement the dark polished concrete floor and white-slat stair.

A bench and white-slat screen separate the entry vestibule from the kitchen, while leading visitors to the living and dining area at the end of the house.

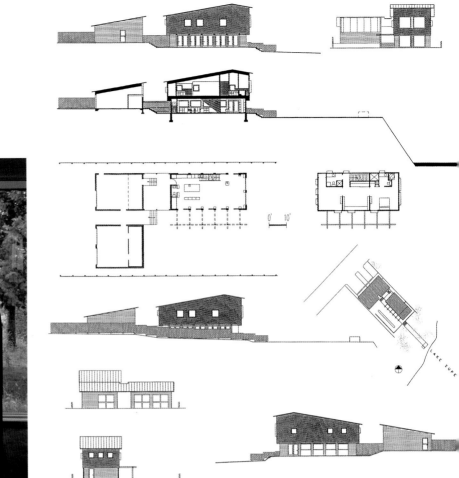

above: An outdoor room, with a fire wall and outdoor furniture on a small terrace, sits on a point of land by the lake, visible beyond the living room's fireplace.

right: As often occurs with Salmela-designed houses, the simplicity of their plans and elevations belies the richness of their materials, colors, and textures.

divisions of the space into sitting, eating, and food-preparation areas. The floor plan leaves much for us to discover. Likewise, the Cotruvos have a collection of classic furniture that others have left behind, from antiques to elegantly modern chairs and tables. Such pieces provide a range of form and color that contrast beautifully with the muted colors—the gray floor, white walls and ceiling, and natural wood bookcases and casework—of the house.

The upstairs has other features left to discover as well. A core of smaller spaces—bathrooms, closets, and the stairway—sit against the north wall, without touching the ends of the house. That one move creates a surprising degree of spaciousness, since the end walls extend beyond your field of vision, making the rooms feel larger than they really are. At the same time, the ceilings rise with the slope of the roof, helping the rooms feel increasingly grand as you move toward the view out the two large windows toward the lake, the greatest asset of the site.

"If the house is ordered enough," says Salmela, "nature provides the asymmetry, the variety." And that approach comes through clearly in the Cotruvo house. Its regular rhythms and repetitions and carefully considered allotments and alignments all highlight the tremendous richness of this once-forgotten location along Lake Superior. This may be a world so many have left, but Salmela has shown in this house the great potential of and real pleasure in repopulating such supposedly marginal land in the city—a world to which so many may one day return.

JOHNSON CABIN

ELY, MINNESOTA

FAMILY HEIRLOOM

above: Set among the trees, this cabin manages to enclose a lot of space within its small footprint, while allowing its elderly owners to live on one floor.

In Minnesota, people love living by one of the state's innumerable lakes, seeing their cabins as cherished property to hand down to future generations, like family heirlooms. The Johnson family is no exception. They owned an existing cabin on Burntside Lake in Ely that stood within the allowable setback from the shore, and they hired David Salmela to renovate the structure and design an addition to it. "The question in such cases," says Salmela, "is what to keep when so much of the cabin was in such bad shape." The Johnsons, advanced in age, wanted to live on one floor, and Salmela provided them with a single, two-story living/dining space overlooking the lake, with a kitchen in one corner, a bedroom in the other, and a bathroom located under the stair. The couple also wanted to leave behind a cabin that their family could use for years to come, and so it has a second-floor mezzanine that contains another bedroom and additional entertaining or sleeping space. Black Skatelite cladding and a metal roof minimize the required maintenance of the exterior. The result is a compact cabin that is ready to accommodate family members of all ages long into the future.

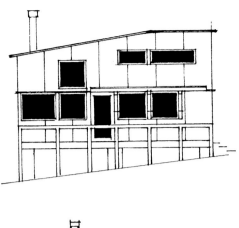

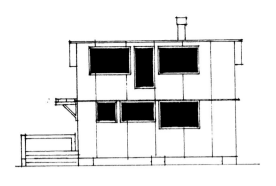

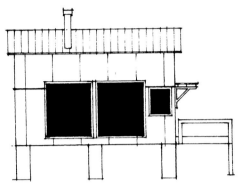

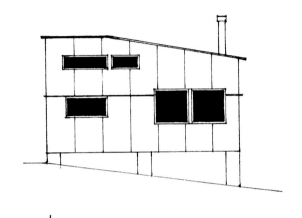

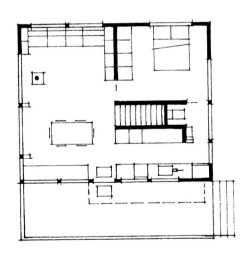

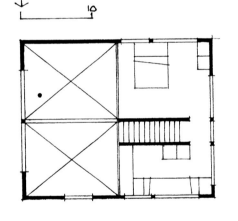

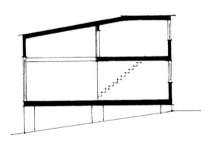

Salmela keeps the cost of such cabins down with simple plans, straightforward elevations, a few materials, and easily built structures.

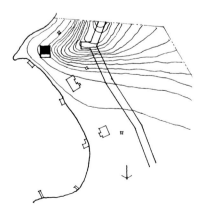

GRAMS CABIN

TWO HARBORS, MINNESOTA

THE LAKE IN YOUR LAP

above: Stretching to face Lake Superior, this house has a long row of large windows with an overhanging roof for protection from the sun, rain, and snow.

Highway 61 threads its way northeast from Duluth to the Canadian border along the shore of Lake Superior, with driveways disappearing down tree-shaded embankments to cabins along the water's edge. The Grams family owned a piece of that north woods and commissioned David Salmela to design a three-bedroom cabin for them. Positioning the house within the allowable setback from the cliff along the lake, Salmela maximized the views of the water by stretching the structure out, parallel to the shore. With a simple, metal-clad shed roof and a cladding of black Skatelite panels and vertical cypress, the cabin has a long bedroom and bathroom wing butted up against a living/dining/kitchen space. "It's like a Scandinavian cabin," says Salmela, "small, tight, and spacious." The living room windows, seven feet wide and eight feet tall, bring the view of Lake Superior through the birch trees right into the house. "It feels like the lake is right in your lap," says Salmela. A large deck stands outside the bedroom wing and leads, via an elevated walk, to a sauna whose shed roof and black cladding echoes the form and material of the main cabin. "We tried to make it as economical as possible," says Salmela, noting the compact plan and maintenance-free exterior materials and landscape. "You don't have to do anything other than vacation there."

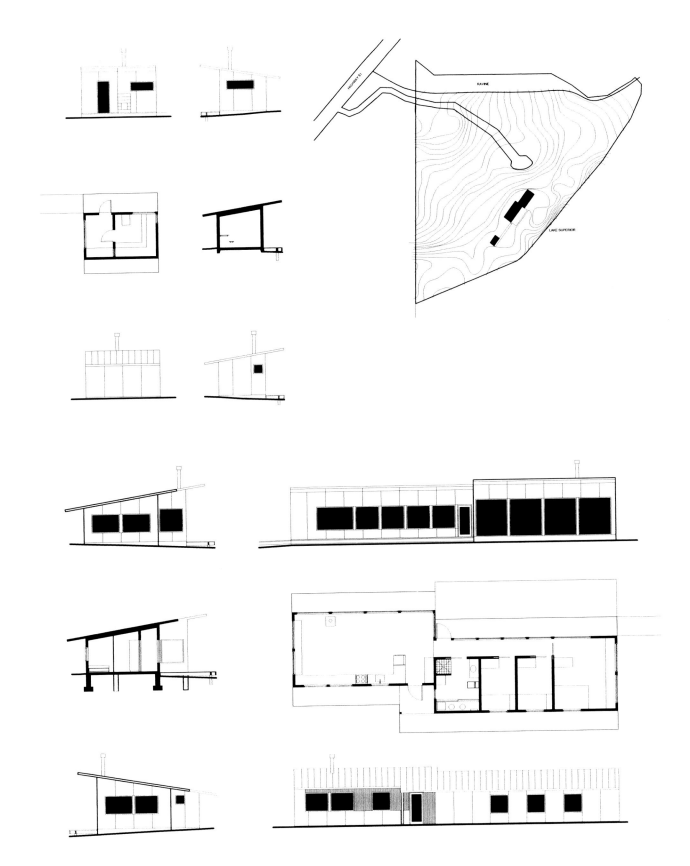

The plan shows how the two wings of the house, one
containing the bedrooms and the other the living area,
adjoin each other, slightly misaligned.

BROGAN HOUSE

STURGEON BAY, WISCONSIN

UP FROM THE ASHES

above: The two-story living and master bedroom wing faces the shoreline, with additional bedrooms and an art studio and recreation room flanking a courtyard.

After the house the Brogan family owned on the shore of Lake Michigan burned to the ground, Julie Brogan saw some of David Salmela's published work in a bookstore in Florida but thought he was "too prestigious," as she says, to design them a new house. But Salmela agreed to do so and "he has been a joy to work with," says Brogan. A working artist, Brogan needed a painting studio as well as bedrooms for her grown children when they visit. The house consists of two wings, with opposed shed roofs that point to the glass-walled entrance link that connects the studio, utility, and recreation spaces to the main house. The two wings "embrace you as you enter," observes Brogan, and they open out to the sand dunes and the lakeshore at the back of the lot. The main house has a wide, skylighted corridor wide enough to serve as a gathering space around the hallway fireplace. At the end of the hall, up a few steps, you come upon the large living room, a dining room and expansive kitchen to your left, and stairs that lead up to a second-floor master bedroom and bathroom suite with commanding views of the water. It's an optimistic house, rising triumphantly from the ashes of a tragic fire.

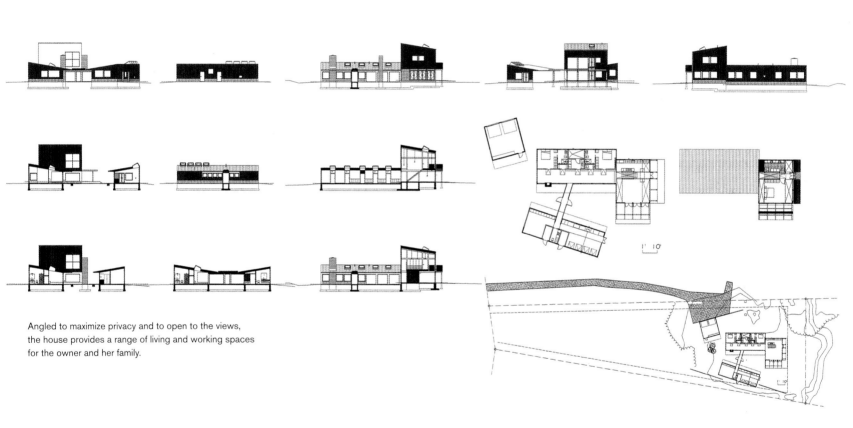

Angled to maximize privacy and to open to the views,
the house provides a range of living and working spaces
for the owner and her family.

TAYLOR WHITEHILL CABIN

DULUTH, MINNESOTA

INCREMENTAL LIVING

above: The alternating shed roofs of the garage and guest cabin echo the scissorslike form of the roof in the main house, with its two-story bedroom wing.

For most of human history, people built incrementally, starting with small structures and enlarging them as they had the need and the means to do so. The cabin David Salmela has designed for the Taylor Whitehall family on the Lester River in Duluth reflects that tradition. The one-car garage and equally sized shop, each with a shed roof sloping in the opposite direction and flanking a wide deck, will be built first, providing a place for the family to stay until the main cabin gets constructed. The shop, with a full bathroom and a sleeping loft, easily doubles as a compact living unit. Eventually, the deck will become a platform that leads to the cabin, which will continue the aesthetic of opposing shed roofs, with standing-seam metal cladding and roofing over a waist-height datum of black Skatelite panels. A bedroom will stand on one side of the cabin's covered breezeway, opposite the main living/dining/kitchen space. A bedroom and bathroom on both the main floor and small second floor complete the plan. The many windows, providing light and views where needed, have a seemingly casual placement that reinforces the incremental idea. According to David Samela, "The shed roofs and asymmetrical windows are an early American idea and a very modern idea, recalling both old barns and Alvar Aalto's Säynätsalo Town Hall."

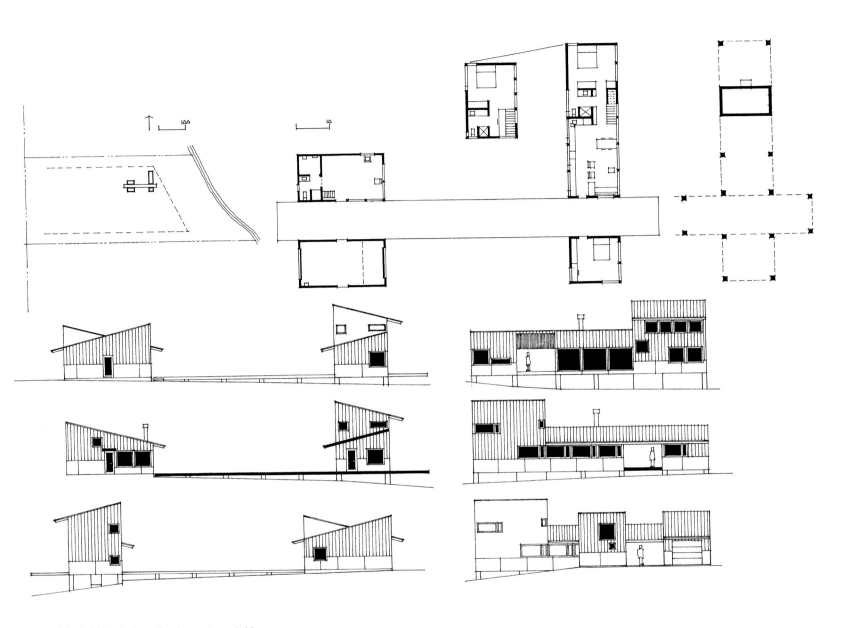

A broad deck divides the house into four parts, maximizing
privacy and providing a variety of places for the family and
their guests to gather.

NELSON HOUSE

DULUTH, MINNESOTA

OWNER BUILT

Houses largely built by their owners often look it, which would have made the house that David Salmela designed for the Nelson family a real standout among do-it-yourself architecture. "The owner," says Salmela, "a very capable Finn, would have done much of the work." Salmela designed the house in three parts—a three-car garage facing a paved court, a shed roof studio for Mrs. Nelson's artwork, and the main structure: a compact, three-floor, shed roof residence shielded from neighbors and the street by a wood fence that turns into a pergola in front of the house. The house's central entry, flanked by a utility room and screened porch on one side and a small kitchen on the other, leads past a straight-run stair to a dining/living room and a recreation space separated by a sliding door. Upstairs, a master bedroom suite, two children's bedrooms, and a bathroom open out to a central gathering space. Downstairs, two additional rooms have south light and access outdoors. The easily built wood-frame structure, with wood trusses spanning its width, has a dynamic exterior, with rows of repetitive windows and planes of different cladding materials—clapboard, plywood panels, and board-and-batten siding—visually sliding past each other. That composition gives the design a striking presence, too striking for the community's developer, who managed to block its being built.

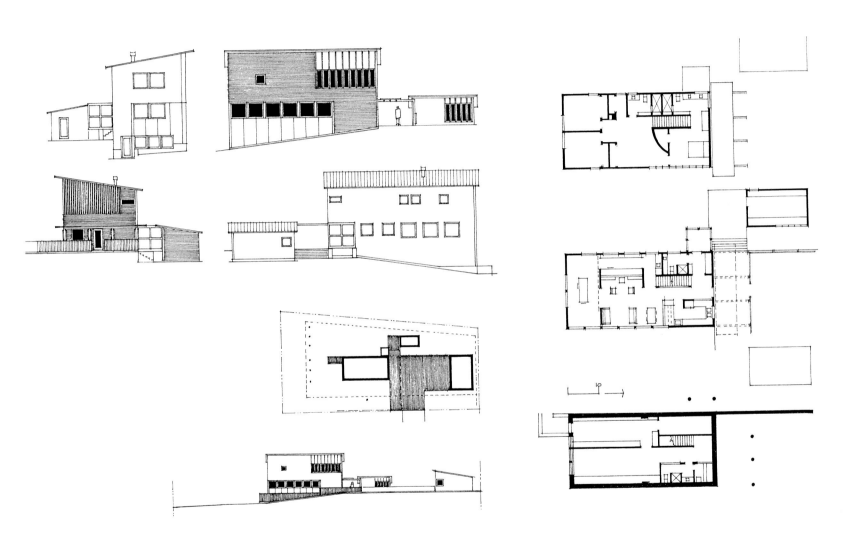

RAMBERG CABIN

GRAND MARAIS, MINNESOTA

TRAIL BLAZING

opposite: The elevations of the house indicate the collagelike quality of its exterior, with a range of materials juxtaposed to reflect its informality.

As our culture has become more high tech, the appeal of the authentic has increased accordingly, leading people to yearn for places like Minnesota's Gunflint Trail, a national scenic byway that winds its way from Lake Superior to the Canadian border. David Salmela's design of a Gunflint Trail cabin for the Ramberg family captures the easy informality of life deep in the North Woods. Located on one of the area's many lakes, the cabin stands on the foundations of an earlier structure, which had a prow pointing south toward the water. Salmela's scheme ensures a number of places to enjoy the outdoors. A broad deck faces east, providing access to the house from the garage and driveway, while a two-story screened porch facing west offers views of the lake and setting sun. Inside, a large living/dining/kitchen space occupies the southern half of the first floor, with a recreation space on the northern end. Upstairs, a master bedroom suite on the north side balances two bedrooms and another recreation room on the south side of the second floor. The down-to-earth quality of the cabin comes through most strongly in its exterior, with its black Skatelite panels, lap cedar siding, and prescribed-burn board-and-batten cladding. "There are fires on the Gunflint Trail," observes Salmela, and this preblackened cabin, complete with solar panels on the roof, looks back-burned and ready for whatever comes its way.

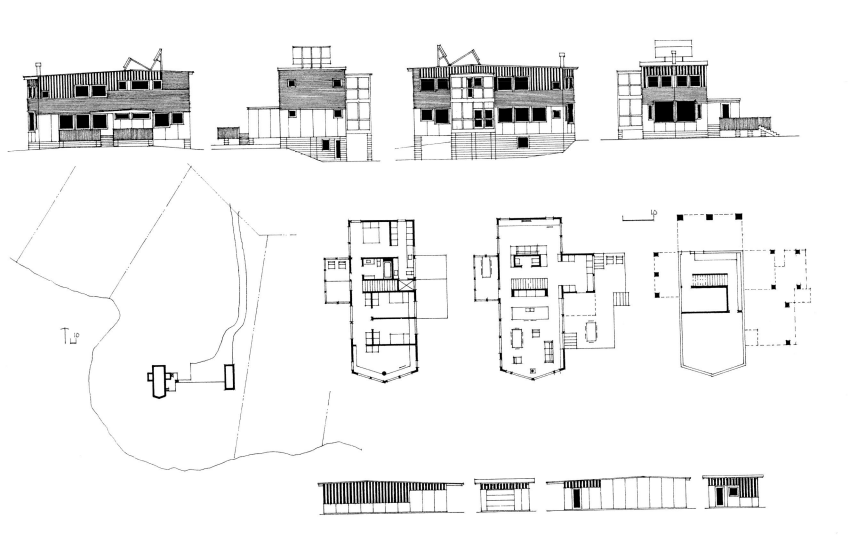

CLUSTERS

COMPOUND INTEREST

We typically think of housing as either single- or multifamily, as something we occupy, on one hand, with family and friends and, on the other, with neighbors whom we may or may not know. In that sense, our housing reflects our society, polarized as it has become between our private lives with close relatives and confidants and the public, composed mostly of citizens and consumers who may remain strangers to us. What often gets lost in such a dichotomy is the vast territory in the middle of these two extremes that is neither completely private nor wholly public, while sharing aspects of both. We all interact with others in this in-between realm, with fellow participants in all sorts of recreational, educational, religious, and other voluntary activities. Such unpaid associations have long been the bulwarks of stable societies, although our cities offer them relatively little space as we have divided the land almost totally between public and private ownership.

Housing offers one opportunity to provide a place for voluntary associations to occur. We can see this in other parts of the world that have developed an array of options between single-family houses and mass housing. Many of these options revolve around the creation of small collections of households whose residents share something in common, ranging from shared cooking in cohousing to shared food production in communes to shared values in intentional communities of all sorts. With fewer units than multifamily housing and greater coherence than single-family neighborhoods, such compounds provide a way in which a small group of families can achieve a scale of community all too rare in our country. The Clure project in Duluth, Minnesota, offers an exceptional example of this kind of community. This development of a few houses, all designed by David Salmela, including one for his own family, reveals the many advantages of living among like-minded people, and the challenges its owners and architect faced in getting it built help explain why such housing doesn't get built more often.

top: The houses in the compound share—and take maximum advantage of—a spectacular view of downtown Duluth, its harbor, and Lake Superior in the distance.

bottom: In winter, the houses, clad in black Skatelite panels, stand as compact forms in their white surroundings, like an arrangement of abstract sculptures on the land.

The Clure project did not begin with a compound in mind. Tom and Patricia Clure bought a piece of tax-forfeited land in 1990 overlooking Duluth's harbor, and they commissioned Cheryl Fosdick, now of CF Design and formerly a partner with David Salmela in Salmela/Fosdick, to design a house for them and one set of their parents. To get utilities to the almost inaccessible site, the Clures bought an adjoining duplex, where they lived during the construction of the new house. When the elderly owner of a small house next door wanted to sell, the Clures also bought that house, and they later purchased the house on the other side of the duplex. "We picked up these properties," says Patricia Clure, "but we didn't want to be landlords, so we started to talk with David Salmela over the years about what we could do with them."

The properties' location made it a particularly difficult problem. Steeply sloped, with a great deal of surface rock, the three parcels faced an alleylike road that ran through the former right-of-way of a railroad incline. At the same time, the passing of their parents left the Clures in a house too large for what they needed. "The idea of doing a progressive, sustainable, urban statement emerged," says David Salmela, although it took years to achieve. They demolished the older houses, and after many meetings with the city, had an approved plan that vacated the street, buried the utilities, rerouted the automobile access, and reconfigured the plats for three new houses. "It's much harder to do urban design," adds Salmela. "You have to get creative within the rules of the system."

Creativity within a set of rules drove the design of the houses as well. "The houses are simple, flat-roofed rectangles," observes Salmela, "with the same siding and flashing details. I could do a hundred houses within those rules and they would all be different." The three houses David Salmela designed—one for the Clures, one for John Morrice and Judith Johnson, and one for himself and his wife, Gladys—all have a remarkable sense of variety within an overall unity. Salmela designed the first house for the Clures, and it became the prototype for the other two. "The Clures wanted a maintenance-free exterior," says Salmela, "and we saw the potential of Skatelite, a locally made, recycled paper-resin composite material used for cutting boards and skateboard parks as siding." To offset the material's integral black color, and to keep water away from the siding's horizontal joints, Salmela used projecting metal flashing at the parapet, lintel, and floor lines that visually ties each of the houses together. Rows of large windows, divided by recycled natural wood jambs, further break up the expanses of black walls, as do the decks' natural wood vertical-slat railings and the garages' white doors and flanking columns.

These exterior elements have the effect of giving coherence not only to each of the three houses but also to the compound as a whole. Historically compounds often had enclosing walls of some kind, but the Clure project achieves that through visual contrast—a set of black houses sitting amid a neighborhood of mostly white ones—and through an imaginative use of the site. The complex has a large outcropping of the Canadian Shield that separates it from the street, and the Salmelas' own house peers out from behind the rock, with a projecting second-floor, wood-slat balcony providing an overlook on the street and a white-painted, concrete-block outdoor chimney standing as a kind of sentinel. Salmela reinforces that sense of being behind a battlement by leading visitors up the back of the rock wall, through a series of concrete steps and timber railings, to a terrace and wide set of stairs up to a covered entry porch. Similar circuitous entrances to the other houses all reinforce the sense of the compound as separate from what surrounds it, while emphasizing the incredible view of Duluth that awaits the visitor once inside the buildings.

Frank Lloyd Wright once said that he never designed a house that did not also imply a new social arrangement, and the same could be said of the Clure project. It offers a set of three, strikingly fresh houses that are visually coherent, simply built, and easily maintained, but it also implies a new social arrangement, one in which community arises from the collaboration of a small group of people. Compounds like this have their challenges: they can take more time to develop, involve more participants needing to agree, and require a level of design greater than the normal subdivision provides. But in an increasingly transient world, in which meaningful relationships with neighbors have become ever harder to sustain over a long period of time, a compound of people committed to being in a particular place may provide one of the best hedges possible against an uncertain future.

The sloping site allows for the accommodation of different houses close to each other, while providing a high degree of privacy and autonomy for each one.

top left: Toward downtown Duluth, the houses have rows of expansive windows that take advantage of the view and visually expand the site into the adjacent open space.

top right: The design blurs the boundaries between houses so that, for example, the wood storage rack for one house attaches to another house for physical stability.

bottom left: By offsetting one house from another, Salmela created outdoor open spaces for each, related to landscape features such as a large tree or rock outcrop.

bottom right: The house farthest down the slope has the garage at the highest elevation, with the main living level a few steps down the hill and bedrooms below.

above: Set amid the outcropping of ledge on the site, the houses in the compound echo the dark color and irregular masses of the rocks around them.

left: Naturally finished wood decks, with wood-slat railings and exterior stairs, give the multistory houses direct access to the land as it drops away.

right: The alley doubles as the driveway for the houses, with stone retaining walls, concrete walks and steps, and wood decks and stairs traversing the slope.

below: The same form, scale, materials, and details link the varied heights and locations of the houses on the site, conveying their sense of unity amid diversity.

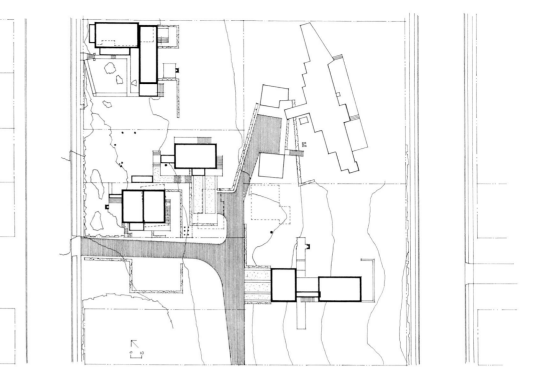

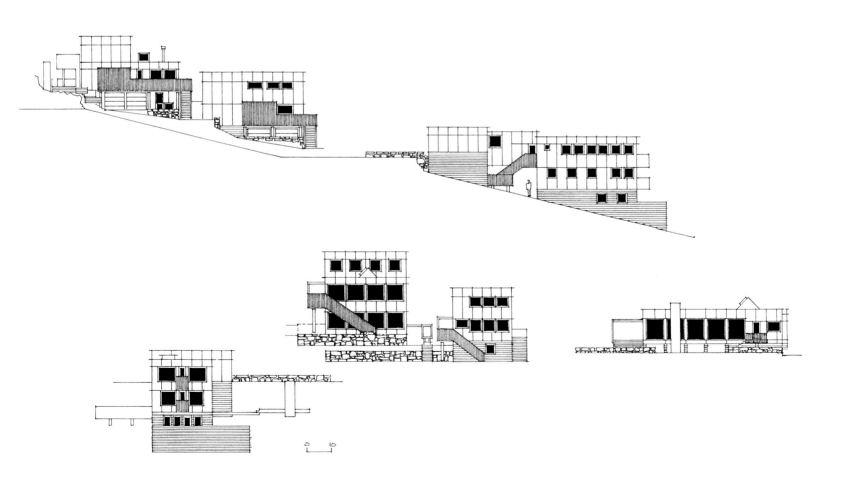

The plans present free-flowing living/dining/
kitchen arrangements and compact bedrooms
and bathrooms.

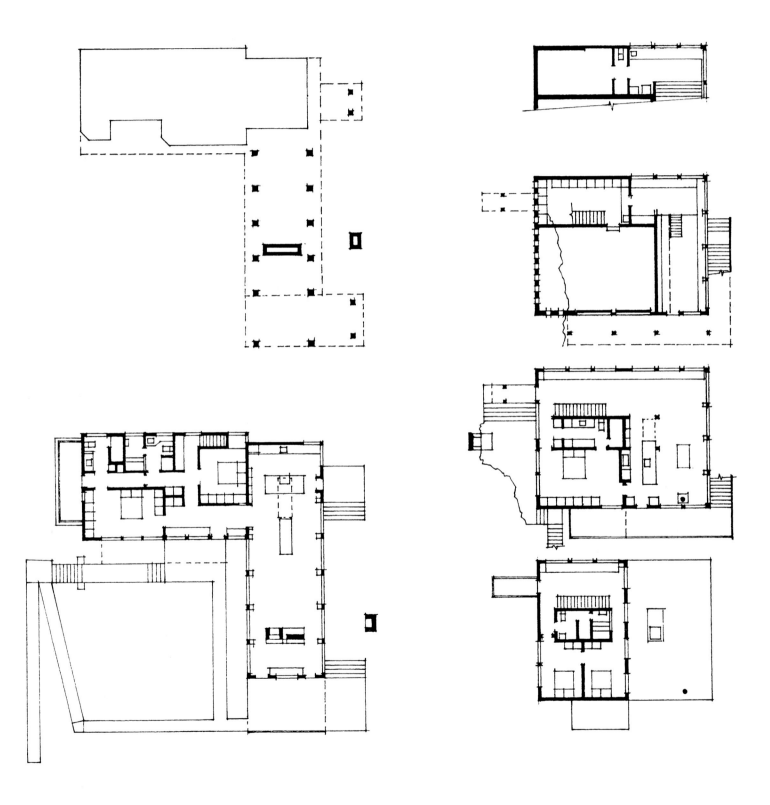

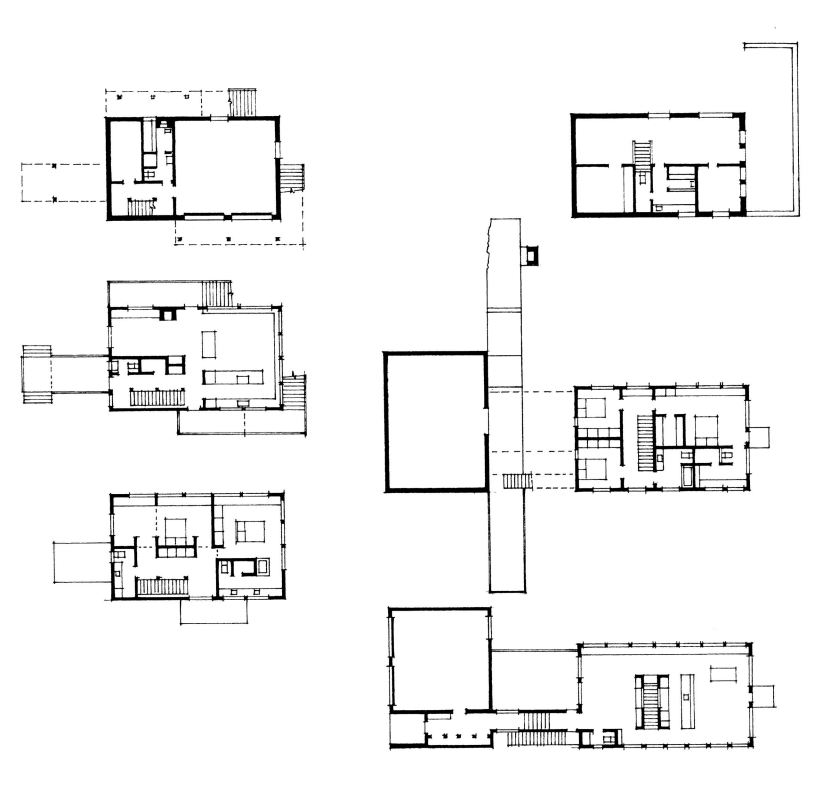

LIVE/WORK/PLAY

Few people live over the store anymore. That once-common integration of our lives with our liveli-hoods has largely disappeared as we have segregated our existence into separate realms of job and family, a division reflected in how we lay out our cities. Through single-use zoning, we have kept different functions physically distinct and often quite distant from each other, resulting in people having long commutes and little time for play between the demands of living and working.

David Salmela's home and office reflects the resistance to this trend that is beginning to grow across North America. Buoyed by digital technology that lets us work from almost any location, increasing numbers of people now work out of their homes or live above their offices. David Salmela does a little of both, showing in his own residence how this reincorporation of our public and private lives can lead to new and more playful forms of living and working.

Most houses separate public and private activities, with living and dining areas kept apart from sleeping and bathing rooms. The return of work to the home, often in the form of the home office, does not easily fit that old formula. Some people let the public invade the private, turning a spare bedroom into an office, while others transform family space into office space, taking over a dining room table for work; either choice can lead to functional conflicts. Salmela's house, in contrast, both integrates and separates public and private pursuits, offering a model of what it means to live above the store in the twenty-first century.

The house occupies a very peculiar site as part of the Clure project. Near downtown Duluth, the fifty-by-one-hundred-foot lot has a large outcropping of rock ledge taking up about a third

Salmela's own house announces the Clure compound from the road with its black form, white chimney, and wood balcony visible behind a rock outcropping.

of the land. At the same time, it offers a spectacular view of Duluth's harbor to the south. "We never get tired of looking at the harbor," says Gladys Salmela. "It's always changing." The ease with which the Salmela house occupies its site, however, belies the skill needed to make it fit. "It took awhile to figure out how to organize the house so that it worked on the site," says Salmela. Some things were given, such as the need to locate the garage at the one relatively level place along the side road. "To make the turn into the garage," Salmela explains, "we needed to pull onto public land." To compensate for that use, he improved the right-of-way by building a beautiful stone retaining wall, installing a gravel parking area, and planting a stand of birch trees, whose plastic protectors around their trunks "look like a Christo," says Salmela.

From the midpoint of the garage in the side of the house, you have two choices. You can follow the stone retaining wall down the slope to the gravel yard and the glass door that leads to Salmela's office or you can take the concrete steps, with their horizontal timber rails, up and over the rock ledge, where you come to a wood deck, an open-face white-painted fireplace, and another set of steps that lead to the front door of the house. The very nature of these dual entries indicates the difference in how this house accommodates both living and working: Salmela gives his home and office their own entrances, equidistant from the point of arrival and as far away as possible from each other.

Clad in durable black Skatelite panels, the house has horizontal bands of projecting aluminum flashing that not only protect the resinous recycled-paper panels from moisture, but also express the layers of functions within: office at the lowest level, garage and office at the midlevel, main living spaces above that, and a guest area at the top. The flashing serves, as well, to lighten the visual heaviness of the dark cladding, providing deep shadow lines that highlight its blackness. Likewise, large windows, white columns, and the natural wood railings and decks that wrap around the house contrast nicely with the black skin.

That contrast becomes even more pronounced on the interior. Whether you enter at the lower level into the light-filled office or at the upper level into the main living areas, you go from a largely black-and-silver exterior to an interior of white walls, expansive aluminum windows, and warm wood trim. The dark-gray tile floors and the deep blue-purple ceiling and central skylight

above: A glass door at grade gives direct access to Salmela's office on the other side of a stone wall, with a gravel parking area on the opposite side of the driveway.

right: The exterior deck and stairs, with their wood-slat railings, shade the large windows that look out from Salmela's office at the lowest level of his house.

over the kitchen further emphasize the brightness and expansiveness of the interior. As you watch the ore boats coming and going in Duluth's harbor below, you sense a similar nautical feel in the house, with its black hull and extensive balconies and stairs encasing a shipshape interior, as white as a sailor's uniform.

David and Gladys Salmela can live entirely on the main floor, with its living, dining, and kitchen areas all in a single large space along the back of the house, and a bedroom, bath, and laundry room along the front. An open wood stair, within its white-painted wood-slat enclosure, leads to a wide upstairs hall, with two bedrooms and a bathroom and sauna, feeling like a captain's quarters on the top deck, complete with a projecting balcony that allows you to look out over the undulating rock to the street below. Down the stairs from the main living level, you come to the garage and mudroom, with space to store outdoor winter gear. The garage holds not only two cars but one of the biggest surprises in the house: the rock ledge on which the structure stands forms part of the garage wall, looking like the hardened lava flow that covered this part of the world eons ago.

Up a step and through another door, you come to Salmela's office. You expect it to be in the basement, having just left the rock-hewn garage, but instead, you come into a story-and-a-half-high room, with a storage balcony up half a flight to your right, and with another slat-railed stair down to the large-windowed office below. Minimally furnished, with a blue-painted conference table, two white chairs, and Salmela's office chair and drafting table by the door, the spare office exudes the modest humility that characterizes much of Salmela's life. Meanwhile, the built-in wood counter, topped with miniature models of recent projects, exemplifies the playful imagination that energizes his work.

above: To get to the front door of the house, guests climb a series of concrete steps (with timber railings), cast next to and on top of the rock ledge front yard.

right: A wood deck, cut around the rock, widens to create an outdoor gathering place with a Salmela-designed wood bench facing the open-ended white chimney.

Having a home and office under one roof not only reduces one's carbon footprint with the shortest possible commute but also enlarges one's life by breaking down the artificial boundaries we have set up between living and working. Salmela's home and office show what great things can come from not separating the two. His integration of work and home has enabled him to add an element of delight to life, something present in all of his buildings and especially evident here, in this home office for serious play.

top left: The simple wood railing up to the front door echoes the elemental form and simple detailing of the bench and the windows and cladding of the house.

top right: Inside the front door you can see back to the fireplace and deck and ahead to the master bedroom and bath, with the stair down to the office at your left.

bottom: Illuminated by large operable windows, a long counter and bench extend the length of the entry vestibule, beside the main staircase with its wood-slat screen.

top: The deep blue ceiling above the kitchen, with its white counters and cabinets, visually separates that space from the living and dining area beyond.

middle left: An office and storage mezzanine overlook Salmela's primary work space, featuring wood-slat railings and screens common elsewhere in the house.

middle right: A counter under the south-facing windows in the office holds the myriad models of Salmela's various projects, most of them also appearing as illustrations in this book.

bottom: Salmela's desk overlooks Duluth's harbor and the other buildings he designed for the Clure compound, allowing him to live and work in and among his creations.

All the elements of an architectural practice—books, files,
models, drawings, computers, and a drafting table—occupy
Salmela's tall, light-filled office.

GAME THEORY

Drive into almost any suburban subdivision, especially one built at the same time by the same developer, and you will see a seemingly endless number of superficial variations of the same few houses. The colors or trim might vary from one house to the next, but you find very little real difference among them. You can choose between the split-level and the colonial, the town-house or the ranch house, but the basic models hardly change. In that way, our housing reflects our larger consumer culture, in which we have endless variations of the same few things and almost no real choice.

Jackson Meadow offers something else: rather than the superficial differences among similar types, it provides a similar appearance of fundamentally different types. Designed by landscape architect Shane Coen and his former business partner, Jon Stumpf, with David Salmela designing all of the houses, Jackson Meadow has an overall uniformity, with certain architectural features shared by all the structures. Every one has the same white-colored wood siding, the same standing-seam metal roof, the same forty-five-degree angle to every gable, the same white windows and doors. The plans also all have the same characteristics: open living, dining, and kitchen areas that flow into each other, sometimes immediately adjacent to each other and other times divided by a stair or an enclosed bathroom and closet.

Even at a detail level, the houses echo one other. Most have ganged windows and doors that open the interior to the outside, and single-loaded rows of bedrooms on the upper levels. And most share the same hardware and handrails, porches and stairs, fireplaces and finishes. In contrast to the standard subdivision, with its superficial variety, Jackson Meadow embraces

above: From a distance, the community looks like a nineteenth-century farming community with a high degree of agreement about aesthetics.

opposite: The density of the development becomes apparent from afar, with a tight cluster of houses in the middle of large open spaces.

an aesthetic commonality. The houses in this development, though, are anything but common. Behind the apparent similarities among houses lies a great deal of real diversity: every house differs in fundamental ways, responding to the varied needs of its inhabitants.

Some houses have separate offices for home workers, others multiple garages for car collectors; some have independent guest suites for extended families, others stand-alone garden sheds for serious cultivators; some have tall studio towers for working artists, others expansive screened porches for nature lovers. These elements, along with a wide range of interior space arrangements, create an almost infinite number of possibilities. In this, Jackson Meadow reflects real life. The standard subdivision assumes that there is a standard family, which hardly exists anymore. Instead, single people, unmarried couples, multigenerational families, and empty nesters are all demographic variations that have become increasingly dominant in recent decades, making the typical nuclear unit of a father and mother with young children less than half the total.

While Jackson Meadow has its share of young families with children—evident in the number of bikes and tricycles seen around the community—the development can accommodate a much wider range of domestic arrangements than typically available elsewhere. At the same time, designers like Coen and Salmela can create a much wider set of options through the standardization of individual elements. This kit-of-parts approach greatly reduces the cost of producing custom responses to people's requirements, and it greatly increases the opportunities of people to get exactly what they need, within a cost they can afford.

But Jackson Meadow shows how getting what we need does not always mean getting what we think we want. Our culture puts a great deal of value on personal expression and individual choice, with the idea that the more we compete, the better off we are. That makes sense if we accept a view of the world as a zero-sum game, in which someone's win means another person's loss. If others are going to impose their wills on us, so should we impose ours on them, with the idea that if we don't, we automatically lose. That view dominated our economic as well as our legal thinking for much of our history as a nation, and politics became a way of balancing the rights of individuals with the good of the community.

Game theorists such as John Nash, who won the Nobel Prize for his work in this area, have changed our view of this dynamic in recent decades. Nash demonstrated that individuals are often better off cooperating than competing, and that what seems to be in our best interest, when seen in isolation, turns out not to be when seen in a larger frame. The so-called prisoner's dilemma provides the classic example of this theory. In this case, two prisoners suspected of a crime can each win a reduced sentence if one tattles on the other and the partner in crime does not. But each will also do much more time if he or she doesn't tell and the partner does. The best overall result for both comes from cooperating with the police and confessing their crime rather than competing with each other and not confessing.

The typical subdivision reflects a win-lose view of the world akin to the prisoner's dilemma, in which individual home owners who try to maximize their advantage to the detriment of others in the development may appear to win a lot at first, but they ultimately lose a lot more in terms of good relations with their neighbors. Jackson Meadow, instead, represents a win-win view of the world. There, individual property owners cooperate with each other in agreeing to moderate their personal expression through their homes in order to achieve a greater good, a more cohesive community, and a more coherent built environment.

While game theory shows us why this approach makes more sense than the constant competition that characterizes American life, it still remains somewhat uncommon and helps explain the reactions Jackson Meadow sometimes receives from those who visit it for the first time. You will hear words like "oppressive" or "monotonous" used to describe the development, as indeed it must seem to those brought up to expect people to maximize their property rights and push their personal expression within the limits allowed by the law. When we have become so accustomed to competition, cooperation can seem odd and certainly unexpected.

It is this goal of cooperation that makes Jackson Meadow so important, not just as a residential development, but as a philosophical one as well. It epitomizes a new way of relating to others by modifying our tendency to put our family's short-term interests and ourselves first, to advance instead the longer-term interest of the community of which we are a part. Because of the mobility

top: Each house has clear property boundaries, but they become impossible to find amid the seemingly informal placement of buildings.

bottom: The repetitive and often smaller windows along the sides of houses contrast with the larger and frequently asymmetrical fenestration on the ends.

of American life, in which people move, on average, as often as every five years, it may not seem to pay to put community before our individual interests, but Jackson Meadow shows the advantage of doing so, even over the short term. By giving up some of their individual freedoms, the residents of Jackson Meadow gain something almost impossible to achieve any other way: a place in which people watch out for each other, care about each other, and work with each other to make the community as healthy and whole as it can be. This isn't game theory; it's the game of life, and one that has sustained humans for most of our history. And if Jackson Meadow is any indication, it may do so again.

IRISH CREAM

top: The shed-roofed alternative has individual bedroom units aligned in a row, next to the main dining hall and kitchen, which serves the whole compound.

above: The gable-roofed version offers varied living arrangements, with some rooms in the main building and attached and dorm-style rooms in outbuildings.

Having commissioned David Salmela to design a retreat for their family, Jim and Colleen Ryan also asked him to create a retreat center on land along the coast of Ireland. The complex, almost monastic in its simplicity, has a series of living units, with a dining hall, gathering space, and a kitchen and mechanical room. Salmela envisioned two schemes. The first has a row of recycled zinc-clad cottages, each with a bathroom, closet, and two single beds beneath a skylighted shed roof, looking out through a large square window to the sea. Near one end of the row of cottages stands a long, flat-roofed masonry building enclosing the common spaces. Here, too, large windows look out to the water, with rows of glass doors along both sides of the tall dining hall leading out to a common terrace. The second scheme has a greater variety of living arrangements, with some hotel-like rooms on a second floor above the shared dining and living spaces, other rooms attached in a separate building under a repetitive row of gable roofs, and two dormitory buildings, each with a row of bunk beds sharing a bathroom. "The first scheme, more modern in its form, is more traditional in how it houses people," observes Salmela, "while the second scheme, more traditional in form, is more modern as housing."

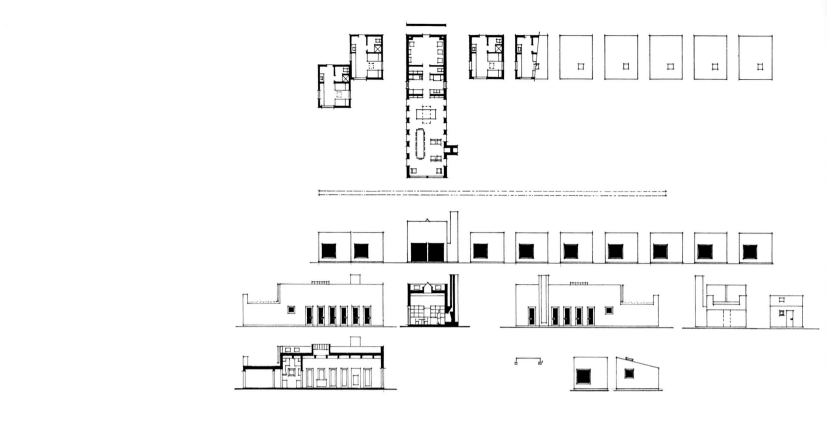

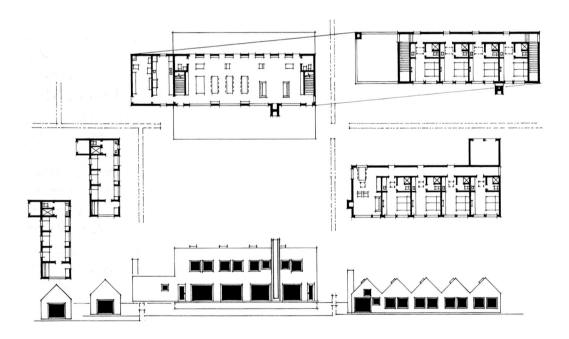

top: With its row of bedroom units, this scheme recalls the minimalist sculpture of Donald Judd and its simple, repetitive, boxlike forms.

bottom: The gable-roofed version offers varied living arrangements, with some rooms in the main building and attached and dorm-style rooms in outbuildings.

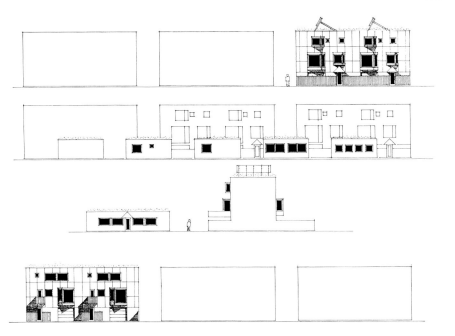

SMALL-TOWN URBANITY

above: To maximize the view of the water, Salmela angles the townhouses' bay windows, while shielding the units from the road with one-story structures.

We don't think of small towns as urban, but they can be, with projects like the development the Bodin family commissioned David Salmela to design on land they owned in Bayfield, Wisconsin. Although it is in an ideal location across from Bayfield's harbor and next to the city's swimming pool, the property is currently a flat gravel lot and is hard to imagine as the diverse collection of buildings and mix of uses that Salmela envisioned there. He has proposed three pairs of townhouses, perpendicular to the harbor, with car access to drive-through garages from the alley. Each unit would have an open living/dining/kitchen space on the second floor and two bedrooms and two bathrooms on the third, with angled windows that direct the view to the water. Across a pedestrian way and along the street, Salmela has placed a set of five, one-story structures that would not block the view of the townhouses behind them and would contain either handicapped-accessible apartments or small professional offices. "This mix of different types of housing and commercial activity used to be more common," observes Salmela, "providing the kind of diversity that small towns need." The various elevation treatments, from green-roofed modern schemes to gable-roofed traditional ones, also reflect the diversity of architecture in towns like Bayfield and reveal the urbanity latent in such small places.

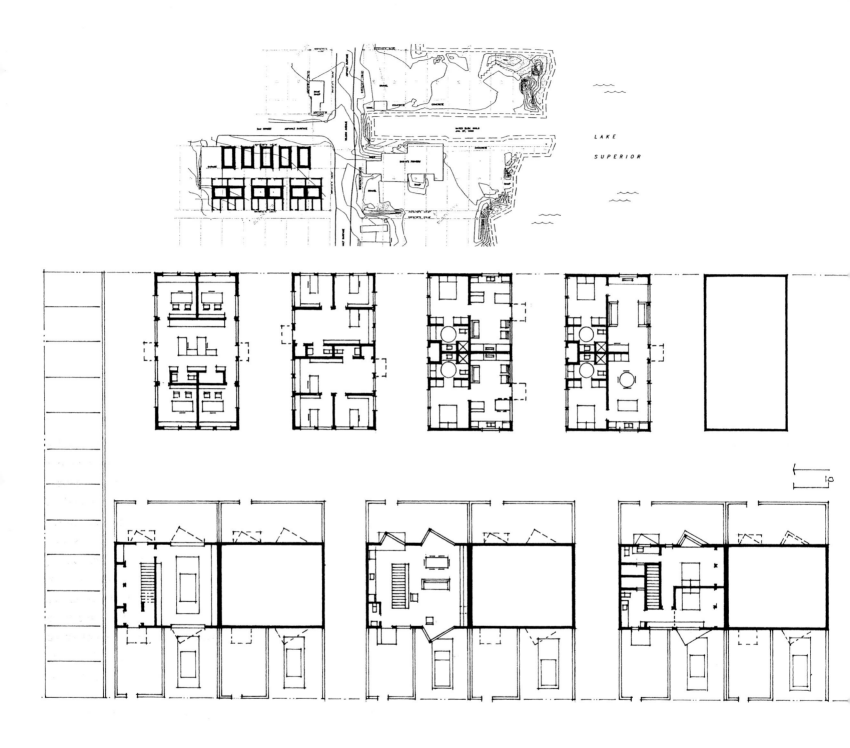

The project creates a dense collection of paired townhouses behind a row of one-story buildings, each able to
accommodate one or two offices or apartments.

DEPOT HILL EQUESTRIAN COMMUNITY

AMENIA, NEW YORK

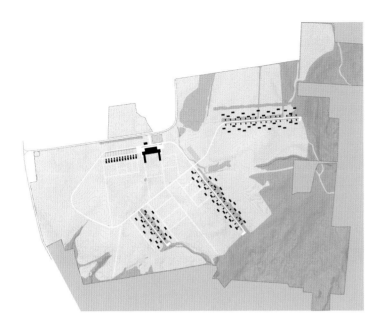

WELL BRED

above: A horse stable (with a line of houses next to it by the road) is the focal point of this development, with its rows of houses along tree-lined streets.

Genetic testing has shown that the modern horse evolved from four prototypical horses in the wild, each adapted to different environments and needs. That idea of a prototype adaptable to a variety of needs underlies the design of the buildings David Salmela has produced as part of an equestrian community the Minneapolis landscape architects Coen + Partners have laid out in the small Hudson River Valley town of Amenia, New York. The large arena and stable building facing the road has a symmetrical plan, with gabled metal roofs over long, single-story wings. A row of twenty-three houses forms a "village" within walking distance of the arena, evoking the rows of houses and garages that Coen located along the tree lines that run between the property's farm fields. Every house, says Salmela, has a "common footprint and materials, including standing-seam metal roofs, black-stained cedar-shingle walls, and clear anodized-aluminum windows." Within that set of rules, Salmela has devised a number of compact, proto-typical plans adapted to the needs of various owners, each with a walkout basement, a living/dining/kitchen space and master bedroom on the main floor, and additional bedrooms on the upper floor. Salmela resisted the pressure in the marketplace to build large structures, knowing that in the design of houses, like the breeding of horses, it's better to be good than big.

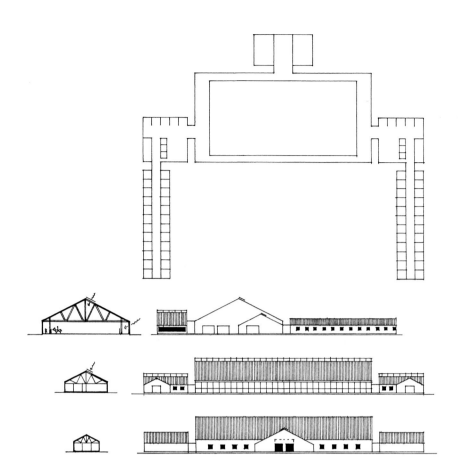

left: The riding facility has two wings of horse stables flanking a central arena, all covered by gabled metal roofs that reflect the local vernacular.

below: Each house demonstrates a variation of the same elements: a narrow gable-roofed form, a walkout basement, a main living level, and bedrooms above.

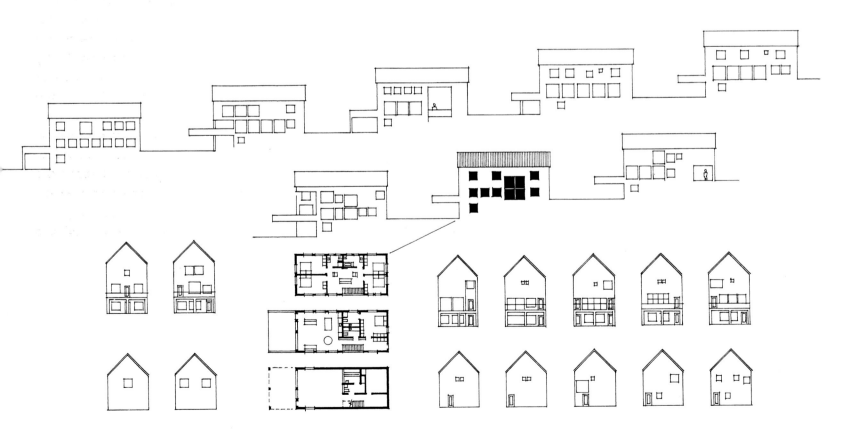

STONEY LONESOME FARM

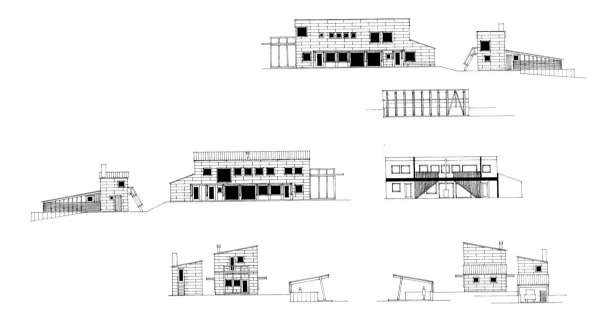

GROWING COMMUNITY

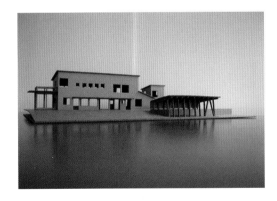

top: The idiosyncratic placement of windows reveals the diversity of activities in the house and in the adjacent outbuildings serving the farm.

above: The shed roof of the main house is repeated in the utility building and garage as well as in the teaching pavilion next to it.

Community-supported agriculture, in which groups of families share in the produce of particular farms, has grown in recent decades as people have sought ways to access healthy food, support local farms, and protect the natural environment, among other reasons. The owners of Stoney Lonesome Farm commissioned David Salmela to design a house, garage and utility building, and an open-air pavilion to teach the families who help support the farm about environmentally friendly ways of growing food. Occupying a promontory facing south, the house consists of a long rectangle, whose kitchen, dining, and living rooms extend most of the length of the first floor, with a screened porch on one end and a study/guest room and bathroom on the other. A pair of opposed stairs leads to four bedrooms above. The shed roofs, metal siding, wood trim, and informal door and window arrangements all evoke, says Salmela, "the barns and sheds in the area." That is especially evident in the teaching pavilion, with its simple shed roof and exposed lumber framing, and the utility building, with its long shed roof over the garage and the two-story mechanical and storage structure. "The owners are very down-to-earth," says Salmela, "and the buildings needed to be as well," suggesting that good architecture has as much a place on a community farm as good environmental stewardship.

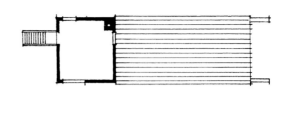

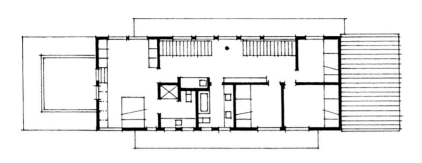

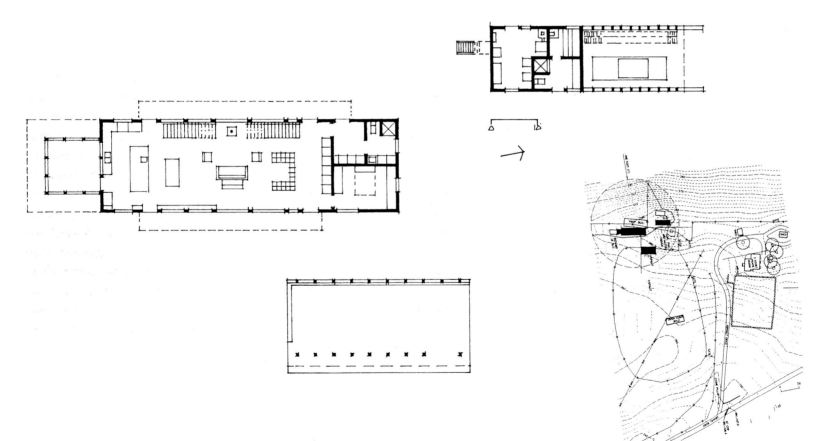

With an almost completely open main level, the house
has a pair of stairs leading to the bedrooms above,
with a screened porch on one end.

FRANCES GRAHAM EQUESTRIAN CENTER

ORONO, MINNESOTA

LIVING WITH HORSES

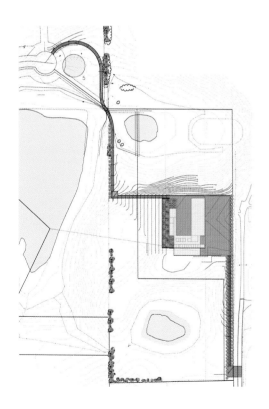

People have long lived with horses when the latter served as our main form of transportation and cultivation. While horses have become mainly recreational animals, the desire to live near them and to be with them remains strong among some people. This equestrian center for Frances Graham, designed by landscape architects Coen + Partners along with David Salmela, reflects that need. Occupying a hilltop site, the center contains a house for the family, a caretaker's house, a four-car garage, stables, and an arena, all arranged around a north-facing court and facing south to a pond. The landscape design, with its two long driveways ascending to the center, has an equally strong architectural form, with lines of trees flanking the mostly right-angle roads, and a bosque of trees and a terrace defining the edge of earthen plinth on which the center and its broad outdoor spaces stand. "The design is very modern, very pragmatic," says Salmela. "The building has a shallow, tapered sod roof, with no more interior volume than is absolutely needed." The connection of the various parts of the center under one roof also enhances the practicality of the center in the cold climate of Minnesota. But, for all its modernity, the center mostly recalls the large house-and-stable complexes that were once common when people lived with—and depended on—horses.

The right-angled roads leading to the outdoor parking and riding areas of the equestrian center recall, in the landscape, the geometry of the building.

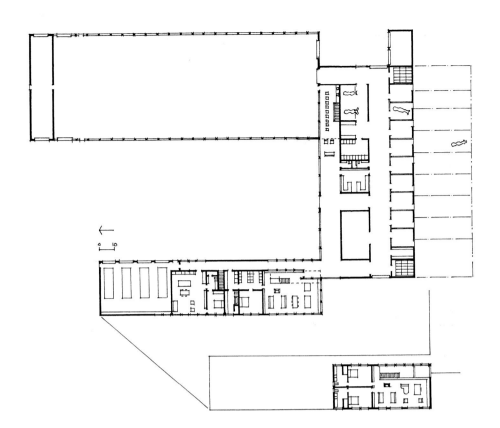

left: The U-shaped plan accommodates, under one roof, a variety of functions, including an arena, stables, offices, lockers, garage, lounge, and living unit.

below: The flat roofs all support vegetation, while clerestory windows and transom lights add to the interior illumination from large windows.

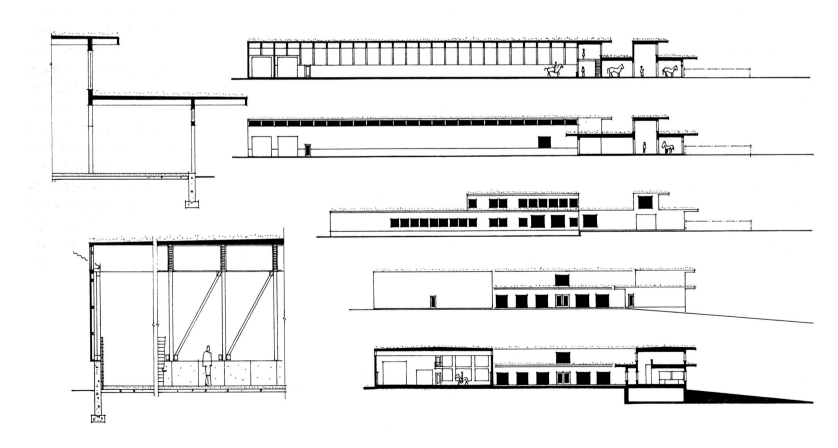

top: Gorgeous stone walls and a wide variety of native grasses give great color and texture to the land and remain among its most memorable features.

bottom: Mowed grass and picket fences define the more urban parts of the development, contrasting with native grasses in the perimeter fields.

top: Houses and garages take full advantage of the undulating topography and patches of woods to minimize the impact of buildings on the land.

bottom: The diversity created within the limited palette of forms and materials at Jackson Meadow becomes clear when seeing houses side by side.

opposite, top to bottom: Elements in the landscape such as fences, trellises, porches, and garages form a common vocabulary among the houses and create intimate spaces.

The amount of land that Shane Coen and Jon Stumpf left in its natural state distinguishes Jackson Meadow from other communities.

Although the houses have extensive areas of glass, they stand far enough apart on the land to give each a great deal of privacy and individuality.

SEMBLANCE OF A WHOLE

"Bits & Pieces Put Together to Present a Semblance of a Whole." That phrase, which the conceptual artist Lawrence Weiner placed as a piece of public art on the exterior face of the Walker Art Center in Minneapolis, captures the way in the which the various parts of the Goldner house became a whole. The house stands at the back corner of Jackson Meadow, along the perimeter road, and it serves mainly as a country retreat from the Goldners' loft in downtown Minneapolis. "This is a getaway for us, and we wanted privacy," says Michael Goldner.

David Salmela, along with landscape architect Shane Coen, achieved that by setting the house toward the back of its site, between two swells in the land. As a result of that placement, the house, on its large rectangular terrace, seems to float on an undulating sea of grass, amidst waves of bluestem and wildflowers. What seems like a single house, though, actually comprises a number of parts. When you approach the house, the slightly curved drive splits into two in front of a pair of single-car garages that form the ends of two separate structures. A swath of gray slate paving extends out from the space between them, beckoning you to come forward. You walk through a narrow paved space between the two buildings into a larger court that looks out to the field of prairie grass beyond the house. The long building to your left, blocking your view of neighboring houses, has a series of doors off the court leading to the guest quarters, mechanical room, and screened porch. To your right, a small, glass-walled office at the back of one of the garages also overlooks the paved patio. "David uses small spaces brilliantly," says Goldner, and this entry sequence demonstrates that statement.

top: Although the house has a mostly glass main living area, its placement at the back of the site, with garages between it and the road, allows a great deal of privacy.

bottom: A stone wall defines the flat front yard, set into the rolling prairie landscape, while birch trees echo the white columns of the wood trellis.

Salmela likes to make clusters of buildings, perhaps recalling the farmsteads he grew up on and lived among as a youth. The Goldner house, however, has many more functions in outbuildings than you often see in Salmela's work. There is efficiency in that approach. In a house used mainly as a weekend retreat, you can close off rooms you don't use without the main house feeling empty. But it also makes you put the parts of the compound together in your mind as you move toward the entrance. Salmela gives you plenty of cues, of course. Once in the court, you have really only one way to go: to your right, under a trellis that runs along the west side of the main house. The trellis shelters a terrace that overlooks a small grass lawn edged with a pristine dry-laid stone wall. Amidst the roughness of the tall grass around it, that lawn provides a welcome bit of civility, like a calm pool beside storm-tossed water.

When you finally arrive at the glass front door and enter the main house, you encounter that same calmness inside. Its various elements—a living room, dining area, and kitchen; a master bedroom and dressing area; a guest as well as a master bathroom; a small office area and banks of closets—all sit, with their requisite doors or enclosures for privacy, within one large space. In this house, you are always aware of the whole. The circulation path around the inside

top: At the back corner of Jackson Meadow, the house faces a terrace, with glass doors in the main house and a screened porch at the end of the service wing.

bottom left: The main house has a master bedroom on one side and a living room and dining/kitchen area on the other, with a core lit by a glass clerestory in the middle.

bottom right: A white masonry chimney divides the living and dining areas, which get their illumination from a row of skylights as well as a wall of windows on both sides.

The perimeter circulation provides views down the length
of the house–from the kitchen, past the living room, to the
office and dressing area beyond it.

above: Like the office area between the bedroom and living room, the bathroom receives daylight through its glass lantern, which also glows from the lights within.

right: The kitchen extends the entire width of the house and has a range of windows, large and small, at different heights to let in light and enhance views.

perimeter of the house reinforces that perception. You enter into a glass-lined hall that flows into the living/dining/kitchen area to your right and the master bedroom/dressing area to your left; you can move along the opposite wall, past a long built-in table that serves as an office, back to where you started.

The spaces that require the most privacy—the bathrooms and laundry area—occupy an enclosure at the center of the house, with a tall, glass, lanternlike structure above them that lets in daylight while providing acoustical isolation "The contractors had a hard time building that clerestory," admits Goldner, "but I like it a lot. It lets in light during the day and glows like a beacon at night." By eliminating the attic and opening up the house to the space under the gable roof, Salmela makes the house seem larger and more connected than it appears in plan. The white-painted wood ceiling, the deeply framed skylights, the heavy timber beams, and the delicate lines of low-voltage lights march down the length of the house and draw your eye up to the airy volume above you. At the same time, the full-height glass walls along the sides of the house draw your eye out to the colorful prairie and distant tree line to the east and to the trim lawn to the west. Salmela and Coen have designed these vistas to maximize the feeling of spaciousness. "I can sit at the dining table," says Goldner, "and look off to the distance without seeing another house," despite the relative density of Jackson Meadow.

Good architecture should delight us, and that clearly has happened here. "Working on this house was the most fun I've had in years," says Goldner. Like many home owners, he seems to take particular pleasure in some of the smallest things: the tiny window above the kitchen sink

The sections indicate the layered quality of the house, with a flat-roof bathroom and utility core sitting within the gabled main house.

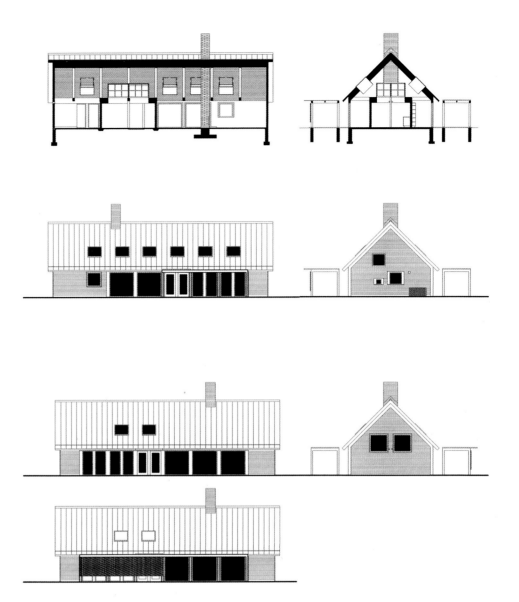

that he can leave open when he is gone, the little fireplace next to the dining table that provides some extra warmth with morning coffee, or the geothermal system that uses the heat from deep in the earth to warm the house. Good architecture should also be a partnership between architect, client, and contractor, and that, too, happened here. "It was a delight," says Goldner, working with the architects and contractors, as they, no doubt, were delighted working with him. "I would not hire Michelangelo and then tell him how to do his sculpture," says Goldner. "I've been a professional long enough myself to know that you have to trust the talent and experience of those you hire."

Good relationships like these demand that we take the time to listen to each other and to talk through what really matters. "At our first meeting with David," says Goldner, "we talked four and half hours!" The artist Lawrence Weiner once said that "without language, there is no art." Without language there also is no architecture, at least no architecture that speaks to people the way Salmela's work often does. And it is through language that architects and clients put the bits and pieces of our lives together into that semblance of a whole we call home.

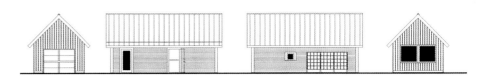

below: The plan shows how the three separate buildings create an urban experience, with a narrow alley leading to a paved plaza with a campanile chimney.

right: The elevations reflect the different functions of each building, with many large windows in the main house and a few small windows in the outbuildings.

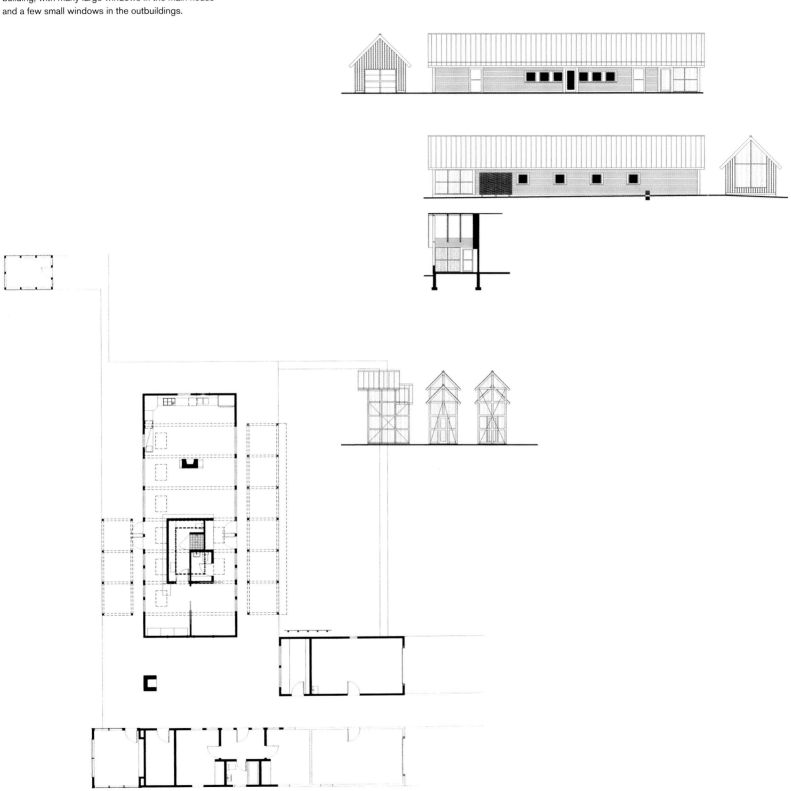

WINTON HOUSE

JACKSON MEADOW, MINNESOTA

SCANDINAVIAN IMMIGRANT ABSTRACTION

above: The three elements of this compound (a garage, guesthouse, and main house) reveal the range of possibilities at Jackson Meadow, from traditional to quirky.

The Wintons have long been patrons of architecture, having commissioned Frank Gehry to design the guesthouse next to their Philip Johnson–designed house, and having hired their own architect son, Nick Winton, to design their loft in Minneapolis. That patronage continued when they asked David Salmela and landscape architect Shane Coen to design a house for them in Jackson Meadow. The two created a compound of buildings, with a freestanding, gable-roofed garage and another garage, part of an L-shaped guest building that defines a grass terrace and provides visual privacy for the main house. Accessed via a terrace and down several steps next to an outdoor chimney, the two-story house has a large glass-walled living, dining, and kitchen space on the main floor, with stairs leading up to a bedroom mezzanine that floats above the living room. "I see this house as the culmination of the modern vernacular vocabulary I've been using," says Salmela, "and I don't know if I can do one better than this one." The Wintons' house certainly deploys a number of the forms and details that have come to characterize Salmela's "Scandinavian immigrant abstraction," as he calls it, from the farmsteadlike cluster of buildings to the steep metal-clad roofs, the unexpected cantilevers, the multiple siding types, the very large and small square windows, and the spare, open interiors.

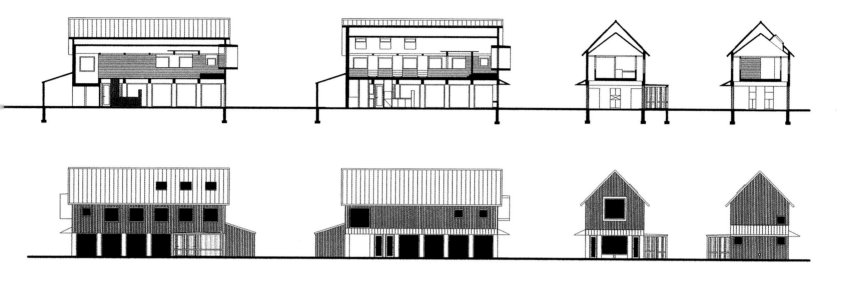

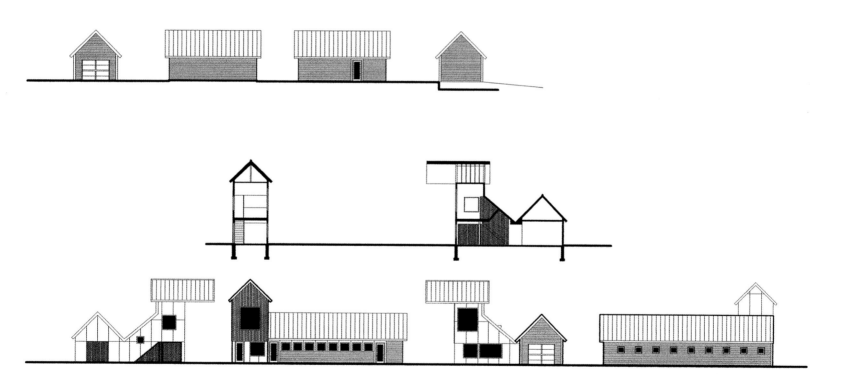

A mezzanine-like master bedroom sits within the two-story
gabled form of the main house, borrowing light from the
windows while maximizing privacy.

The house steps down the hill so that the main house
at the back of the lot has a great deal of privacy, shielded
from the road by the garage and guesthouse.

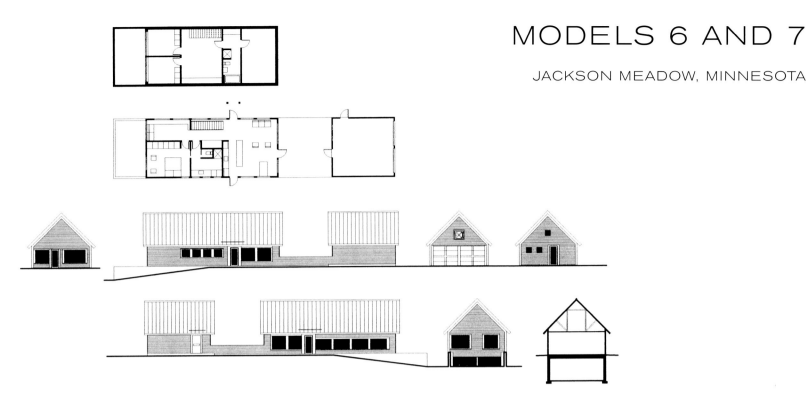

MODEL MODESTY

above: This one-story house with a walkout basement proves that a lower-cost structure is feasible within the rules at Jackson Meadow.

Although the houses of Jackson Meadow remain relatively modest in size in comparison to the megamansions that have cropped up at the outer edges of cities around the United States, David Salmela's houses in that development can cost more than most people can afford. As a result, he has developed a couple of model houses that fit the architectural vocabulary and site design standards of Jackson Meadow, while offering a much less costly option for people of more modest means who want to live in the community. Model 6 consists of a one-story, gable-roofed house and garage of equal width, with a walled yard between them that constitutes the only landscaping on the site. The main level of the house has an open living/dining area, with a kitchen between them and a master bedroom. Downstairs, bedrooms and a recreation space look out to a lower light court. Model 7 offers a two-story version, with a separate garage. This model consists of a simple rectangle, with a kitchen/dining space separated from the living room and its corner office by a straight-run stair that leads to a lower-level recreation space and basement and an upper floor of three bedrooms and two bathrooms, joined by a large hallway with floor-to-ceiling glass windows at both ends. "Even modest houses need a mood-setting space like that," says Salmela.

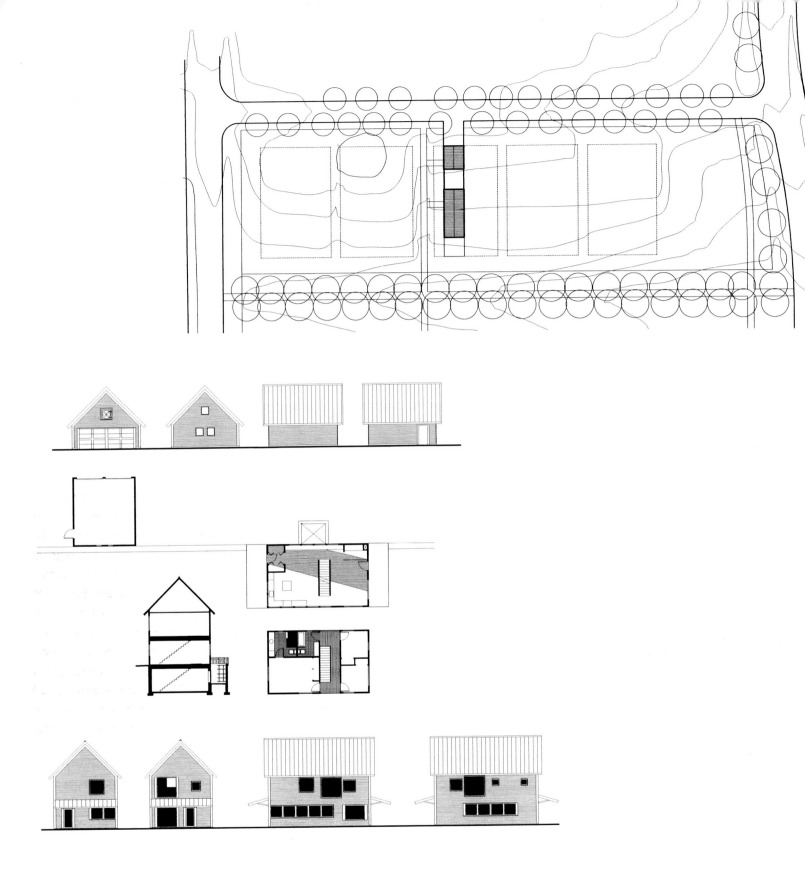

A two-story option also exists. A stair serves as the
room divider on the first floor, with three bedrooms
and two bathrooms on the floor above.

DORSEY CREEK RANCH

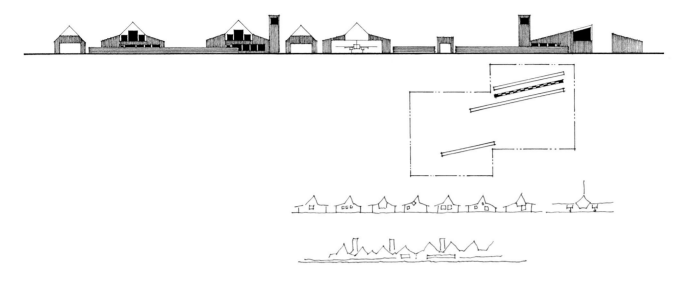

FLY IN

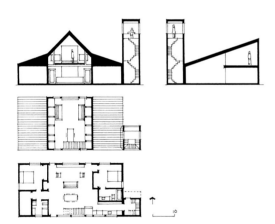

This fly-in development presents a mix of housing, garages, and airplane hangars, which share the same cladding and single- and double-pitch gable roofs.

Architecture may be as different from aeronautics as possible, with the one involving heavy, fixed structures and the other light, mobile machines. But that difference seems less apparent and less relevant in this "fly in" retreat that David Salmela and landscape architect Shane Coen have designed for a client in Wyoming. "We thought of it as the anti-Aspen," says Salmela. Providing a place for pilots and their families to fly to relax and be with other plane enthusiasts, the development consists of eighty lots adjacent to an airstrip. Salmela has envisioned the houses having airplanelike roofs, with a high central tail-like gable and shallower winglike roofs spreading out to either side. That evocation of the airplane's form has functional as well as symbolic reasons, since some of the structures would serve as houses for the owner and others as hangars for the planes. The row of gable and shed roof houses, garages, and hangars also recalls the peaks of the Big Horn and Rocky Mountain ranges to either side of the development. To help residents watch the coming and going of planes and enjoy the surrounding landscape, Salmela has also designed viewing towers as an option for home owners. The houses themselves, with bedroom/bathroom suites around shared living/dining/kitchen spaces, could accommodate families or unrelated friends flying in for extended periods of time or for short stays: architecture for the aerodynamic.

237 Dorsey Creek Ranch

AWARDS

2010
Residential Architect Award, Grand—Yingst Retreat and Pavilion

2009
Architectural Record/Business Week Honor Award—Hawks Boots Factory

2008
AIA Minnesota Gold Medal
National AIA Housing Award—Streeter House
Residential Architect Award, Grand—Streeter House
AIA Minnesota Honor Award—Yingst Residence
AIA Minnesota Honor Award—Hawks Boots Factory
AIA Minnesota Honor Award—Mayo Woodlands, with Coen + Partners & Altus Architects

2007
Honorary Doctorate of Humane Letters, University of Minnesota
AIA Minnesota Honor Award—Clure Project

2006
American Architecture Award—Streeter House
Home of the Year Award, *Architecture* Magazine—Streeter House

2005
National AIA Honor Award for Architecture—Emerson Sauna
National AIA Honor Award for Urban Design—Jackson Meadow, with Coen + Stumpf
Residential Architect Award, Merit—Matthew House
AIA Minnesota Honor Award—Wild Rice Restaurant
AIA Minnesota Honor Award—Streeter House

2004
Architect of Distinction Award, AIA Minnesota/ *Midwest Home*
Phaidon Atlas of Contemporary World Architecture—Emerson Sauna
American Architecture Award—Emerson Sauna
Wood Design Award, Citation—Jackson Meadow
AIA Minnesota Honor Award—Matthew House
National American Society of Landscape Architects Award—Mayo Woodlands, with Coen + Partners and Altus Architects

2003
Wood Design Award, Merit—Emerson Sauna
AIA Minnesota Honor Award—Emerson Sauna

2002
Inducted into College of Fellows, FAIA
Wood Design Award, Merit—Albrecht Residence
Wood Design Award, Citation—Jones Farmstead

2001
National American Society of Landscape Architects Award—Jackson Meadow, with Coen + Partners

2000
National AIA/PIA Community Design Award—Jackson Meadow, with Coen + Stumpf
National AIA Louise Bethlune Award for Photography— "Walter Netsch" photo
AIA Minnesota Honor Award—Jones Farmstead

1999
AIA Minnesota Honor Award—Jackson Meadow, with Coen + Stumpf
AIA Minnesota Honor Award—John Franks Sauna

1998
National AIA Honor Award for Architecture—Brandenburg's Ravenwood Studio
Architectural Record House—Emerson Residence
American Wood Council Award, Merit—Brandenburg's Ravenwood Studio

1997
AIA Minnesota Honor Award—Brandenburg's Ravenwood Studio
AIA Minnesota Honor Award—Gooseberry Falls Visitors Center

1996
AIA Minnesota Honor Award—Emerson Residence

1995
AIA Minnesota Honor Award—Carlson Outbuildings

1994
American Wood Council Award, Citation—Loken Residence
AIA Western Red Cedar Honor Award—Loken Residence
AIA Minnesota Honor Award—Hanson Retreat

1993
AIA Minnesota Honor Award—Loken Residence

1991
AIA Minnesota Honor Award—Smith Residence

1990
AIA Minnesota Honor Award—Thompson Residence (while with DSPB)

1987
AIA Minnesota Honor Award—Scott Kerze Cabin (while with DSPB)

1985
AIA Minnesota Honor Award—Wick Residence (while with DSPB)

BUILDING CREDITS

STREETER HOUSE
Deephaven, Minnesota, 2005
Client Kevin Streeter
Architect Team David Salmela, FAIA; Carly Coulson,
AIA; Souliyhan Keobounpheng, AIA; Scott Muellner
Landscape Architect Coen + Partners
Structural Engineer Bruno Franck
Contractor Streeter & Associates

HAWKS BOOTS FACTORY
Duluth, Minnesota, 2008
Clients Greg Benson, David Benson, and Tony Ciardelli
Architect Team David Salmela, FAIA; Carly Coulson, AIA
Structural Engineer Jim Berry
Contractor Johnson Wilson Constructors

CHRISMER CABIN
Ellison Bay, Wisconsin, 2008
Clients Robert and Alice Chrismer
Architect Team David Salmela, FAIA; Malini Srivastava,
AIA
Structural Engineer MBJ
Contractor Highview Builders

RYAN RETREAT (MAPLE SPRING)
Mellen, Wisconsin, 2009
Clients Mike and Pam Ryan
Architect Team David Salmela, FAIA; Carly Coulson, AIA
Landscape Architect Coen + Partners
Structural Engineer Jim Berry
Contractor Craig Quimby

STREETER JOB SITE TRAILER
2008
Client Streeter & Associates
Architect Team David Salmela, FAIA
Contractor Streeter & Associates

STREETER MODEL HOME
2006
Client Streeter & Associates
Architect Team David Salmela, FAIA
Contractor Streeter & Associates

BAGLEY NATURE PAVILION
Duluth, Minnesota, 2010
Client University of Minnesota
Architect Team David Salmela, FAIA; Carly Coulson, AIA
Structural Engineer MBJ
Mechanical Engineer Gausman & Moore
Electrical Engineer Gausman & Moore
Civil Engineer Salo Engineering
Energy Consultant Conservation Technology
Contractor University of Minnesota

KRAUSE CABIN
Ely, Minnesota, 2010
Clients Brian and Lisa Krause
Architect Team David Salmela, FAIA; Malini Srivastava,
AIA; Tia Salmela Keobounpheng; Souliyahn
Keobounpheng, AIA
Structural Engineer MBJ
Contractor Rod & Sons Carpentry

HYYTINEN CABIN
Cook, Minnesota, 2010
Clients Jon and Shelley Hyytinen
Architect Team David Salmela, FAIA; Malini Srivastava,
AIA
Structural Engineer MBJ
Contractor Rod & Sons Carpentry

SINGLETON HILL HOUSE
Minneapolis, Minnesota, 2008
Clients Tracy Singleton and Dana Hill
Architect Team David Salmela, FAIA
Landscape Architect Close Landscape Architecture

FRYKHOLM PHILLIPS HOUSE
Grand Rapids, Michigan, 2007
Clients Steve Frykholm and Nancy Phillips
Architect Team David Salmela, FAIA
Landscape Architect Coen + Partners

ZAMZOW HOUSE
Duluth, Minnesota, 2009
Clients Joel and Kris Zamzow
Architect Team David Salmela, FAIA; Malini Srivastava,
AIA
Structural Engineer MBJ

CAFESJIAN TOWER
Roseville, Minnesota, 2008
Architect Team David Salmela, FAIA

KOCH CABIN
Little Marais, Minnesota, 2008
Clients Charles and Kathy Koch
Architect Team David Salmela, FAIA; Malini Srivastava,
AIA; Tia Salmela Keobounpheng
Structural Engineer MBJ
Contractor Rod & Sons Carpentry

KEEL CABIN
Makinen, Minnesota, 2007
Clients Mary and Karl Keel
Architect Team David Salmela, FAIA; Souliyahn
Keobounpheng, AIA
Contractor Rod & Sons Carpentry

ANDERSON HOUSE
Bayfield, Wisconsin, 2003
Clients John and Mary Anderson
Architect Team David Salmela, FAIA; Souliyahn
Keobounpheng, AIA
Landscape Architect Coen + Partners
Contractor Bayfield Construction

DELOIA HOUSE
Duluth, Minnesota, 2008
Clients Gary and Linda Deloia
Architect Team David Salmela, FAIA; Carly Coulson, AIA
Landscape Architect Coen + Partners
Contractor Bell's Remodeling

ARVOLD HOUSE
Duluth, Minnesota, 2003
Clients David and Judy Arvold
Architect Team David Salmela, FAIA; Souliyahn
Keobounpheng, AIA
Landscape Architect Coen + Partners
Contractor Rod & Sons Carpentry

RYAN CABIN
Gilbert, Minnesota, 2009
Clients Jim and Colleen Ryan
Architect Team David Salmela, FAIA; Carly Coulson, AIA
Structural Engineer MBJ
Landscape Architect Close Landscape Architecture
Contractor Rod & Sons Carpentry

JOHNSON HEDLUND HOUSE
Duluth, Minnesota, 2010
Clients Paul Johnson and Laura Hedlund
Architect Team David Salmela, FAIA; Malini Srivastava,
AIA
Structural Engineer MBJ
Contractor Rod & Sons Carpentry

ANDERSON LANDSCAPE AND SAUNA
Duluth, Minnesota, 2009
Clients John and Mary Anderson
Architect Team David Salmela, FAIA; Carly Coulson,
AIA; Souliyahn Keobounpheng, AIA; Tia Salmela
Keobounpheng
Structural Engineer MBJ
Contractor Bruckelmyer Brothers Construction

HOLMES PROTOTYPE CABIN
Ely, Minnesota, 2005
Client Rod & Sons Carpentry
Architect Team David Salmela, FAIA
Contractor Rod & Sons Carpentry

FIORE CABIN
Ellison Bay, Wisconsin, 2010
Clients Michael and Beth Fiore
Architect Team David Salmela, FAIA; Malini Srivastava,
AIA
Structural Engineer MBJ
Contractor Highview Builders

JORGENSON SUNDQUIST HOUSE
Deephaven, Minnesota, 2010
Clients Jerry Sundquist and Rebecca Jorgenson
Sundquist
Architect Team David Salmela, FAIA; Malini Srivastava,
AIA
Landscape Architect Coen + Partners
Structural Engineer MBJ
Contractor Sahlstrom Construction

COUNTRY HOUSE
Marine on St. Croix, Minnesota, 2005
Architect Team David Salmela, FAIA
Landscape Architect Coen + Partners

GOLOB FREEMAN CABIN
La Pointe, Wisconsin, 2004
Clients Bruce Golob and Jean Freeman
Architect Team David Salmela, FAIA; Souliyahn
Keoboupheng, AIA; Tia Salmela Keobounpheng
Landscape Architect Coen + Partners
Structural Engineer Bruno Franck
Contractor Northwoods Construction

MATTHEW CABIN
Brainerd, Minnesota, 2004
Clients David and Kathy Matthew
Architect Team David Salmela, FAIA; Souliyahn
Keobounpheng; John Lintula
Landscape Architect Coen + Partners
Contractor Majka Construction

YINGST RETREAT AND PAVILION
Empire, Michigan, 2009
Clients Doug and Bonnie Yingst
Architect Team David Salmela, FAIA; Carly Coulson, AIA
Landscape Architect Coen + Partners
Structural Engineer Jim Berry & Bruno Franck
Contractor James Anderson Builders

SCHIFMAN HOUSE
Minneapolis, Minnesota, 2010
Clients Jim and Lissie Schifman
Architect Team David Salmela, FAIA; Malini Srivastava,
AIA; Tia Salmela Keobounpheng
Landscape Architect Coen + Partners
Structural Engineer MBJ
Contractor Streeter & Associates

ODEH HOUSE
Rochester, Minnesota, 2008
Clients Diya and Eman Odeh
Architect Team David Salmela, FAIA; Malini Srivastava,
AIA
Landscape Architect Coen + Partners
Structural Engineer MBJ

ROLAND CABINS
La Pointe, Wisconsin, 2009
Clients Chris and Helen Roland
Architect Team David Salmela, FAIA; Carly Coulson,
AIA; Tia Salmela Keobounpheng
Structural Engineer MBJ
Contractor Northwoods Construction

COTRUVO HOUSE
Duluth, Minnesota, 2003
Clients Tom and Christina Cotruvo
Architect Team David Salmela, FAIA; Souliyahn
Keobounpheng, AIA
Landscape Architect Coen + Partners
Structural Engineer Bruno Franck
Contractor Rod & Sons Carpentry

JOHNSON CABIN
Ely, Minnesota, 2009
Clients Corky and Lyle Johnson
Architect Team David Salmela, FAIA; Malini Srivastava,
AIA; Tia Salmela Keobounpheng
Structural Engineer MBJ
Contractor Rod & Sons Carpentry

GRAMS CABIN
Two Harbors, Minnesota, 2009
Clients John and Kathy Grams
Architect Team David Salmela, FAIA; Malini Srivastava,
AIA
Structural Engineer MBJ
Contractor Rod & Sons Carpentry

BROGAN HOUSE
Sturgeon Bay, Wisconsin, 2010
Client Julie Brogan
Architect Team David Salmela, FAIA; Carly Coulson, AIA
Structural Engineer MBJ
Contractor Borkovetz Building & Supply

TAYLOR WHITEHILL CABIN
Duluth, Minnesota, 2010
Clients Matt Whitehill and Kate Taylor
Architect Team David Salmela, FAIA; Souliyahn
Keobounpheng
Structural Engineer MBJ
Contractor Owner

NELSON HOUSE
Duluth, Minnesota, 2007
Clients Mark and Mona Nelson
Architect Team David Salmela, FAIA; Carly Coulson, AIA
Structural Engineer MBJ

RAMBERG CABIN
Grand Marais, Minnesota, 2010
Clients Stephen and Kathryn Ramberg
Architect Team David Salmela, FAIA; Carly Coulson, AIA
Structural Engineer MBJ
Contractor Lande Construction

CLURE PROJECT
Duluth, Minnesota, 2008
Clients Tom and Patricia Clure
John Morrice and Judith Johnson
David and Gladys Salmela
Architect Team David Salmela, FAIA
Structural Engineer Jim Berry
Contractor Rod & Sons Carpentry

SALMELA HOUSE
Duluth, Minnesota, 2008
Clients David and Gladys Salmela
Architect Team David Salmela, FAIA
Structural Engineer Jim Berry
Contractor Rod & Sons Carpentry

JACKSON MEADOW
Marine on St. Croix, Minnesota, 1999–2010
Client Jackson Meadow Company
Planning, Architect, Landscape Architect Salmela
Architect; Coen + Stumpf; Coen + Partners; David
Salmela, FAIA; Jon Stumpf, ASLA; Shane Coen,
ASLA; Souliyahn Keobounpheng, AIA; Nathan
Anderson; Travis Van Liere; Stephanie Grotta; Brian
Kramer
Structural Engineer Bruno Franck
Wetland Engineer RLK
Contractor Cates Construction; Anderson Sorenson
Homes; Streeter & Associates

GOLDNER HOUSE
Jackson Meadow, 2006
Clients Mike and Barbara Goldner
Architect Team David Salmela, FAIA; Malini Srivastava,
AIA
Landscape Architect Coen + Partners
Structural Engineer MBJ
Contractor Streeter & Associates

WINTON HOUSE
Jackson Meadow, 2006
Clients Mike and Penny Winton
Architect Team David Salmela, FAIA; Malini Srivastava,
AIA
Landscape Architect Coen + Partners

MODELS 6 AND 7
Jackson Meadow, 2008
Architect Team David Salmela, FAIA; Malini Srivastava,
AIA

IRELAND RETREAT
Ireland, 2009
Clients Jim and Colleen Ryan
Architect Team David Salmela, FAIA

BODIN DEVELOPMENT
Bayfield, Wisconsin, 2007
Architect Team David Salmela, FAIA; Carly Coulson, AIA

DEPOT HILL EQUESTRIAN COMMUNITY
Amenia, New York, 2007
Architect Team David Salmela, FAIA
Master Planners and Landscape Architect Coen +
Partners

STONEY LONESOME FARM
Gainesville, Virginia, 2009
Clients Pablo Elliott and Esther Mendelheim
Architect Team David Salmela, FAIA;

FRANCES GRAHAM EQUESTRIAN
CENTER
Orono, Minnesota, 2006
Client Frances Graham
Architect Team David Salmela, FAIA
Master Planners and Landscape Architect Coen +
Partners

DORSEY CREEK RANCH
Basin, Wyoming, 2008
Client Robert Elliott
Architect Team David Salmela, FAIA
Master Planners and Landscape Architect Coen +
Partners

David Salmela, FAIA, is the principal architect in the firm Salmela Architect in Duluth, Minnesota. Since 1985, his projects have received forty-nine regional and national awards, including three National AIA Honor Awards.

Thomas Fisher is a professor in the School of Architecture and dean of the College of Design at the University of Minnesota. He is author of *In the Scheme of Things: Alternative Thinking on the Practice of Architecture* (Minnesota, 2000); *Salmela Architect* (Minnesota, 2005); *Lake/ Flato Buildings and Landscapes; Architectural Design and Ethics: Tools for Survival;* and *Ethics for Architects,* and coeditor of *Designing for Designers: Lessons Learned from Schools of Architecture.*

Peter Bastianelli-Kerze is an artist living in Eveleth, Minnesota. His architectural photographs have been published in more than a dozen books as well as in numerous magazines, including *Abitare, Architecture, Architectural Record,* and *Architectural Review,* and his work has been exhibited at the Cantor Arts Center at Stanford University. He has been honored for his exceptional photography by the Minnesota AIA.